The Carin' Sharin
By Dave Gu

With cartoons by Simon Kewer

A Prose from Dover (UK) book

Published by Digest Publishing

All these articles were previously featured in The Rider's Digest
between February 2000 and July 2002 (issues 30 to 58)

Printed by Print for All, London, England

Digest Publishing Ltd
PO Box 45358
London
SE14 5ZP

Contents

Introduction

I first met Dave Gurman at the beginning of 2000 after he had sent me an article for possible publication in The Rider's Digest, a motorcycle magazine I had created a few years earlier for the London motorcycle courier community.

It was fated that Dave should become involved in TRD given his history in the courier trade. As a rider for Mercury Despatch in the late seventies and early eighties, Dave worked the streets of London at a time when the courier industry was beginning to find its feet. Dave's stories of the people, the bikes, the crazy riding tell of a time of free-wheeling, big money earning where there seemed no limit to the possibilities and motorcycling was central to everything.

Dave's first contribution, International Rescue – a story about how a group rode from London to France to help repair the storm damage done to a friend's farm – was a perfect complement to the existing editorial, entertaining and written in a style that engaged the reader with the story being told. From there, it was an obvious step for Dave to become a regular columnist.

Although writing comes easily to Dave, as his former editor and friend, I do feel a small sense of pride in helping him develop over the years. Many times we have argued over the finer points of punctuation, grammar, and most of all, length of article. Editing other people's work is not easy at the best of times and Dave has had to come up with many a convincing reason as to why I shouldn't excise entire paragraphs in order to get the whole to fit the pages I had allocated. One memorable issue had Dave arriving at my house on the Saturday morning after deadline in order to edit his monthly contribution as he absolutely refused to let me do it. For one hour he sat at the computer, excising a word here, altering a phrase to make it shorter. He had to remove something like 500 words – the best part of page – but managed to do it, in time, and without damaging the flow. It was a masterful piece of editing.

The Carin' Sharin' Chronicles show the many faces of Dave Gurman, his love of motorcycles (the late seventies Ducati 900SS above all), redheads, music, and making people laugh, think and question in equal parts. Some of them ramble and others you will read and wonder what it's actually all about but it all becomes clear by the end. That's one of Dave's greatest skills. Whatever he writes, you always want to see how it ends.

I'll finish this introduction with one of Dave's own quotes which not only manages to describe how so many motorcyclists feel about their chosen form of transport but encapsulates in a phrase Dave's ability to tap into the psyche of his readers: *"A biker is someone who rides through choice. Not because it is the most comfortable way to transport a body but because it can be the most magical way to carry a soul."*

Roger Tuson
Founding Publisher/Editor
of The Rider's Digest

Preface

Before 1993 it had never occurred to me that I would ever write anything aside from letters. I'd been a voracious reader since I was a child and I'd always been more than happy to join in any verbal discussion, but every school report I ever received commented on my almost pathological inability to translate my oral contributions into words on paper; then, around eighteen months before my fortieth birthday, I suddenly developed a desperate need to do just that. However, I didn't start writing at that portentous period in my life because I felt an urgent necessity to communicate my pain to my fellow man, no, my reason for putting fingers to keyboard was altogether more prosaic.

In April 1993 my friend Rich Newton was an established car photographer who was doing lots of work for *Car* magazine. When he rang me out of the blue to ask if I'd like a couple of days' work driving 'something tasty' while he took some snaps, he knew it was an offer I couldn't refuse. What he really meant was would I be able to arrange the time off at such short notice? I said yes instantly, then phoned my boss and promised all sorts of trade-offs, and cashed in a whole stack of goodwill and favours to make good on my word – and two days later I was driving west at dawn with the stereo banging in a brand new Audi S4. My 'work' involved driving to Weston-super-mare to meet up with another four cars for a five vehicle shoot on the beach (which led in turn to a little recreational racing on the sands with the local tearaways afterwards); an overnight in a four star hotel followed by an entertaining drive to Crickhowell, where we then shot a series of action pics on a lovely twisty bit of Welsh mountain road before heading back to London. It was the realisation that for the professional journalists on the job it had been just another couple of days' work that prompted me to start writing. I didn't have any aspirations to have a book published; all I wanted was enough leverage to be able to borrow cars and bikes for jollies.

It was almost seven years before I felt ready to submit anything and when Roger responded by saying the article I'd sent him (*The Spring of my Discontent*) was "engaging – but too long for the Digest" I quickly dashed off something shorter. Then a strange thing happened; once I had a regular slot in the mag, my ambitions regarding the scrounging of motorcycles seemed to take a pillion seat, while I got carried away with the whole idea of having the opportunity to get my tuppence worth across in print.

All these articles originate from a two-and-a-half year period that kicks off with my first contribution to The Rider's Digest in February 2000 and finishes in the summer of 2002 – a few months short of my first proper ride on a press bike. When these words were written TRD was entirely aimed at couriers working in and around the capital; and although they all rode motorcycles, they were quite a separate and distinct group, with their own particular brand of humour. Alan Ainsworth's comment on the back cover is a perfect illustration, as is the following quote from my second Digest article (which didn't make it into this book): -

"My name is Dave. My surname is no more important now than it was when I started in the despatch business in 1978. Back then, when there was a need to differentiate between me and all the other Daves, I was Dave 23. These days, in certain biking circles I carry the tag Caring Sharing Dave – or Carin' Sharin' for short. However this is not solely because I'm a warm lovely human being, who'll happily give his last Rolo to anyone. It actually refers to the fact that since totting-up prompted a break from despatching in 1982, I've been working more or less solidly as a residential social worker (with the very teenagers the Daily Snail will assure you are the problem with the world today). Of course I didn't get the moniker as affectionate recognition for all the wonderful work I've done over the years; in the best despatch riding tradition it originally comes from an old Alexi Sayle sketch, where he rages at, "Caring sharing Dave the fucking social worker... C*NT!!" and helpfully suggests, "Help a London child... Kill a social worker!" Despatch riders, don't you just love their sense of humour?"

The target audience also accounts for occasional despatch business jargon. I did consider adding footnotes to clarify some of the more obscure terms, but I decided that there really weren't that many that they would render the tales unintelligible – even for a reader with zero comprehension of the world of motorcycle couriers – and the stories would flow better if I didn't distract the reader with unnecessary explanations. Hopefully you'll agree; because I'm pretty confident that this volume contains more than enough common points of reference for anybody with a passing interest in motorcycles – or, dare I say, life in general – to relate to.

Dave Gurman, October 2008

Acknowledgements

I would never have got around to putting this compilation together if it hadn't been for the illumination, encouragement and inspiration provided by Simon Kewer and his fantastic witty cartoons – thanks a bunch Si.

Thanks also to Rich Newton for introducing me to the whole idea of writing; to John Burton for reading the first thing I wrote for public consumption and offering supportive constructive criticism ever since; to Roger Tuson for giving me my first break; to Mark Mathewson for bringing the same kind of excellent design and layout values to this book as he has to every Rider's Digest since issue 8; to Linda Gilby for her proofing work on both; to Glenys Armstrong for kicking off the project proper by editing the first half dozen articles; extra big hugs and kisses to the ever luscious Liz Anfield for casting her thoroughly educated eye over the remainder and excising the worst of my punctuational excesses (in spite of being seriously irritated by at least one of the pieces); and to Paul Blezard – the nit-nurse of the editing process and a perfect illustration that there's nothing like an old pro!

An extra special mention for my mother Sylvia who will be ever so happy and proud that this book was published in time for me to give her a copy for her 80th birthday (even if she won't admit it within my earshot); and my 'children' Sam, Matt, Nick and Joe, who know that they are everything that is really important in my life.

Last but not least I'd like to express my eternal gratitude to all the motorcyclists generally and couriers in particular, who contributed to the experiences that I've described in the following pages – I can't imagine what I would have written about without you. I hope a few of you recognise yourselves and enjoy my account.

International Rescue
TRD issue 30 – February 2000

The top news story when I sent my first contribution to the Digest in February '00, was the government's latest attempt to gag ex-spy David Shayler, after he 'blew the whistle' on shady MI5 operations. He provided the Mail on Sunday with "damning details" of the spooks' operations, the most serious of which being the accusation that the government kept secret files on politicians who had by then become cabinet ministers.

Shayler had been in "political exile" in France ever since the revelations were first published in August 1997. Having been unsuccessful in their 1998 attempt to extradite him, the government took out a civil writ accusing him of breaches of confidence and contract and of breaking copyright laws.

Personally I could never understand the Law Lords' refusal to accept his defence that he was acting in the public interest. What sort of logic considers it wrong to inform the population that a dodgy government department has been spying on their democratically elected politicians?

International Rescue

At first glance you'd be forgiven for wondering what the hell this story – heartwarming as it may be – is doing in the Riders Digest. Any association with the despatch business is at best tangential and it's not even directly about bikes. But it is about bikers.

I've ridden bikes since I bought my first one – a secondhand Suzuki TS90 – in 1975. Across the quarter century betwixt then and now there have been many magic times, including my first bout in the courier business (starting at Mercury in '78) and, from 1981 to '83, owning and enjoying a 1979 black & gold Ducati 900SS. However high points aside, the one constant that's made me happy – and proud – to be a biker, is the feeling of comradeship.

I'm sure a lot of people reading this are about to skip to the next article (or advert even), convinced I'm simply a fogey on a nostalgia trip. That I need to get real. There may or may not have been some sort of brotherhood way back in some imagined golden age, but this is Y2K. We've had the Gimme Eighties and the Nasty Nineties and nobody really gives a toss anymore. Given the amount of peace, love and harmony around in Year Zero, it might just as well be the *Khmer Rouge* running things!

I realise we live in a meaner, harsher world, but the Sixties weren't all Californian sunshine and light. Besides all the usual nastiness and petty rivalries that continue to spark violence among bikers today, back then you had two tribes who believed that the difference between their wheel sizes, riding position and dress sense justified them beating the shit out of each other. Which they did regularly – with boots, bottles and motorbike chains – whenever they met by chance or by special appointment over Bank Holidays. Even when you put Mods & Rockers aside, bikes (and parts of them) have always been stolen; road rage has always existed (except in those days, car starter handles were more common weapons than krooklocks); and there have always been pathetic wankers on bikes who are worse than car drivers for intentionally blocking your progress through traffic.

But so what if the world is an infinitely more wicked and less caring place, it's all relative. As a biker you are still more likely to be on the receiving end of a random act of friendliness, kindness or support from a brother or sister of the road, than any car driver, pedestrian, or public transport traveller. If you've broken down or need a little help and other motorcyclists are aware of the situation, you will still find people stopping to offer assistance. And in moments of real despair there's no greater sight than a friendly biker pulling up to check if they can help.

The most lonesome I've ever felt was in the middle of the day, sitting in a gutter alongside my crumpled bike in the Royal docks. In 1976 the area was a wasteland and I squatted there in a short sleeved t-shirt, oozing claret from a large hole in my left elbow for over fifteen minutes. One or two cars a minute slowed down to manouver around the bike and have a quick shufty, but not a single one stopped. Just as I was begining to slide into despondency, I heard the rasp of a two stroke coming fast, the first bike since I dumped it. My first instinct was to warn the rider of the diesel slick I'd discovered, but he saw me as he came round the first bend and braked immediately. He jumped off his RD200, picked up my bike and put it on the pavement before turning to me and saying, "Fuck me, that's gotta smart!" He bunged me on the back of his bike and dropped me down the road at the "Seaman's Hospital", before zipping off saying, "Gotta rush, I was already late back from lunch... Good luck!" And he was gone in a puff of blue smoke.

Working on the same principle, the last weekend in January, four crusty bikers who've all seen the back of forty climbed into Thunderbird 2 (an aging, but spacious green Montego turbo-diesel estate, with an ever so slightly leaky head) and set off to France for a bit of international rescue. The only difference was that on this occasion we weren't heading out to pick up a CX500 with a knackered cam chain, or a mangled Le Mans with matching rider – but we were on a mission to rescue a biker in despair.

For years Ash ran an adventure playground in Thamesmead and was at the same time a well known figure on the southeast London bike scene. About seven years ago, having had it with the rat race, he and his lady, Jane, sold their flat in Deptford and bought a small farm in Normandy. So nowadays Ash and Jane are doing the "*Good Life*" bit and he spends more time on a horse than a bike – but he's still a biker at heart. It's fortunate then that their farm near Vire is an ideal staging post en route from London to Le Mans. Over the years, dozens of after-work travellers have ridden to Ash & Jane's farm and crashed out; knowing they'd wake in the morning refreshed and enjoy a top breakfast before setting off on the relatively short blast to the circuit.

So in recognition of years of sterling service to international biking, when the word went out that the folks at La Fosse (literally "the ditch") were in trouble we scrambled into action. OK, so it took a month to get it together, but the Tracy brothers don't have day jobs or kids; and they've also got clever hydraulic systems that whoosh them straight into their seats, and swimming pools that slide open!

We didn't choose the pot-bellied rescue craft because we couldn't deal with the prospect of a cold ride; if all Ash needed was some biking friends to pat him on the back and mellow him out, we'd have zipped over on our bikes (although to be honest the nippy ten degrees below that was registering when we arrived at 4am on Friday morning isn't really my idea of a fun-filled bike ride), but it wasn't simply the reassurance of seeing friendly faces that was needed. What was required was chain saws and muscle.

As you may or may not be aware France received an extra special Xmas pressie this year. In the wee small hours of December 25th, a storm swept through the country that made the one we had here in '87 seem like we'd left our trees in a nasty draught. Now I'm sure there are quite a few people out there who think it's a good job, that it's no more than the beef-banning snailmunchers deserve; but, besides being just a tad xenophobic, it also ignores the fact that Ash is a sarf London boy! And to hear how two days after his 40th birthday, he lost one-and-a-half barns and around 30 trees would melt even a controller's heart.

Walking around the farm seeing little aside from destruction and debris brought to mind the DR parties we'd enjoyed in Peckham twenty years earlier – only Ash didn't even get to have any fun messing his farm up. But it reminded me how in the past enough people with black bags – even people with terminal hangovers – can make a hell of a dent in the most daunting of shit heaps. So in spite of the crisp weather we were soon stripped to lumberjack shirts (suspendies and a bra... oops!) and chopping fallen trees in a manner that would have done Tobe Hooper proud.

In the two-and-a-half days we had to work, we were able to clear little more than a field and a bit, but like any overwhelming task, it's the getting started that's the hard part. By the time we said our farewells on Sunday we'd given Ash and Jane a good head start, and more significantly we'd reminded them that if you're a biker you're never completely alone.

Empathy may not be a word that's overused in the rufty tufty world of motorcycles, but if you've been riding a bike for any period of time you can't help knowing how that other person feels and what you gonna do, drive past? Or am I just an anachronistic idealist? Is it really just a few aging riders who still believe in a "Do unto others as you would have done unto you" school of biking? If you've never thought to do it before, next time you see a rider with a problem, check it out, you never know what simple thing could make all the difference. It feels brilliant to be rescued, but not half as good as the glow you get when you ride away knowing that just for a moment there, you were the milkman of human kindness.

Be careful out there
Carin' Sharin' Dave

Reasons to be Cheerful
TRD issue 32 – April 2000

The big story internationally was the snatch of a six-year-old Cuban shipwreck survivor by a Miami SWAT team, but aside from demonstrating just how bizarre life in America can be, it held little resonance for me.

The story that really stopped my clock, cut off my telephone, prevented the dog from barking with a juicy bone, and silenced the pianos, was the tragic – but not altogether unexpected – death of Ian Dury who I describe in a P.S. at the end of the following article as, "a first rate geezer and possibly the greatest ever peoples' poet".

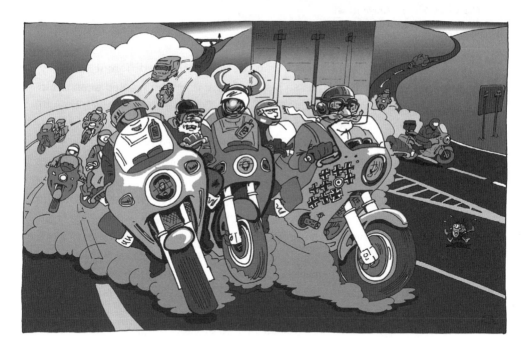

Reasons to be Cheerful

Last month's description of a low-key reunion of old Mercury bods covered the *who*, *where* and *when* at great length, but it scarcely touched on the *WHY?* Why were there still so many people willing to go to so much effort to meet up after all these years?

Nostalgia is defined in my dictionary as a "sentimental yearning for a period of the past". If that's the case, the halcyon days we were all aching for must have come somewhere in the first decade of the courier business proper: between about '72 and '82. Which is not to suggest that the people who turned up spend their lives longing for a bygone age – most of them probably rarely give it a thought – but once it comes up, they still find it difficult not to grin.

Of course I did mention the why at the end, but it was almost a toss-away – you could say I skimmed over it like a knee across tarmac. Excuse the trashy bike mag cliché, but in a way it sums up what Mercury was all about: riding bikes. It was that simple. We were working there because we loved bikes and they paid us passable wages (+ overtime) to ride them all day long – and then let us take them home at night. What more could a boy reasonably ask for?

In the Seventies we were living in an entirely different country. Unemployment was negligble, so just about anyone who wanted a job could get one. There was no such thing as 'Care In The Community' back then; if you were capable of walking out of a psychiatric hospital, you could get a job at a British Rail Red Star office. In that climate, few people went into the despatch business because it was the only way they could put a roof over their head and a jam butty on the table.

My affection for those days isn't about our youth – we were all sorts of ages from teens to thirties – it was the industry that was young. Prior to dispatching, the average biker (i.e. me) had to make do with a fun ride to work on an old bike, followed by eight to ten hours in a shop, factory, workshop or warehouse, before having another blast on the way home. The idea of being paid to ride a pretty new bike all day was more than most lads' wildest imaginations stretched to. The fact that we were working was almost secondary; as long as the jobs were all cleared quick enough, you were free to do whatever you wanted.

For me the job was just like a fantasy only better. Each morning when I got on the bike and called in using the helmet mounted transmitter/receiver, I got an enormous buzz. It was pot luck, anything could happen. I felt like a WWII fighter ace. Every day offered me fresh opportunities to mainline adrenaline whilst dicing with real mortal danger. Admittedly the Messerschmitts and Fokkers had been replaced by buses and Post Office vans, but the principle was the same – albeit rarely quite as terminal. I loved it; the freedom, the risk, the variety and, even then, some drop-dead gorgeous receptionists. But more important than all that, I thrived on the feeling of camaraderie.

Twenty years ago, when we went out en masse we were a swarm of orange. Whether it was a party, an *Evidence* gig, a game of football, or a late-night curry, we shouted our common identity. At that time it would have been obvious to anyone walking down the Broadway that a large group had assembled in NW7 and they'd be in no doubt about who the mob were.

The ride home would kick off one of two ways: there was the sensible consensus and the Le Mans start; but ultimately how we began was irrelevant, because it would always end the same way – balls out. We'd scream across town in a manner that would have me tutting with disgust these days, murmuring about accidents looking for a good spot to happen.

Actually there was the third way to ride off, which was particularly popular outside the *Alfred* in the summer months, and that was the comical turn. These were always good for a laugh, sometimes even for the person unwittingly providing the entertainment. There was a weird mentality at Mercury in those days, which seemed to reason that as we were riding company bikes, it was OK to fuck about with them. Unfortunately this combined with a generally shared "anything for a laugh" disposition that displayed a worrying lack of concern for the bodies involved.

Most of the people laughing loudly at Luigi's were there when Woffy wheelied down Castellain Rd, bouncing off cars when his Vaselined left handlebar grip came away in his hand. But at least he managed not to dump it, so he returned to the whistles and applause of his "mates". Which is more than you could say for the poor buggers who had their right hand panniers filled with water; all they got when they fell over pulling away were jeers and wanker signs.

On one occasion we tried to get a bike's engine to run backwards. We were talking in the cafe about the fact that it was supposedly possible to bump-start a two-stroke in reverse. The idea of getting someone to give it a big handful, unaware that their bike – which would be sitting in neutral with the engine running – would launch them in the wrong direction, was irresistible. When a rider turned up and dashed off to the Press centre for a slash, there were four of us laughing maniacally while desperately bumping his GT down the ramp alongside Luigi's cafe. We dropped the bike twice, but fortunately knew nothing about timing, so we didn't manage to pull it off. Milky's idea, inspired by the Burt Reynolds movie *Hooper*, involved fixing a cable with a lot of slack to someone's bike, while the other end was tied to a lamppost. It wasn't followed up due to the lack of a suitable cable, rather than any sensible consideration of the potential dangers.

The zenith of the Mercury social scene was a barbecue party hosted by the Dover office in the Summer of '79. Around twenty bikes and half a dozen or so vans, with pillions and passengers assembled in two groups north and south of the river. I was in a courtyard in SE15, waiting with a load of others for a van driver to finish his Saturday morning run, when the crew at base in Maida Vale set off for the Blackwall tunnel. The controller kept us (and other riders who joined them en route) updated on their progress and they were well on their way before our convoy burst rudely onto Peckham High St.

In spite of some outrageous driving by our two vans, as the boys and girls from W9 sailed past Bromley-by-Bow, we were still bogged down in the Blackheath Road and looking very dodgy for our synchronised rendezvous at the *Sun In The Sands* roundabout. We upped the ante and took some appalling liberties, which I couldn't begin to describe here just in case the statute of limitations hasn't run out on them. Suffice to say, we reached the roundabout above the A102(M) flat out, with the other bunch only half way through their second circuit; so we slotted straight in and joined them for another couple of pannier scrapers before peeling off towards the coast. Anyone who's seen the film *Taras Bulba*, will remember the Cossack hordes galloping across the Steppes with their numbers swelling along the way; well it was kinda like that only on a slightly smaller scale – and in orange.

The ride down was a blast, every time we reached a roundabout the bikes entered first and shut it down, only giving way to the vans. We avoided unnecessary stops by refuelling on the move; the occupants of the vans passed opened cans and bottles, unwrapped choccy bars and lit cigarettes out to the bikes, who then handed them on like relay batons (joints however were definitely not circulated in this way, as at 85-90mph, the fags were burning down at an alarming rate). The party was nearly as much fun as the ride down there – and probably just as dangerous. All round it was a truly memorable event.

The social and working scene all blurred into one. Work was a series of chance encounters with mates, where you'd meet, mess about for a while, then shoot off on your separate ways. Most of the regular contract runs had been clocked and any rider who fancied himself would have a tilt at the record. On a few occasions half the fleet would be poodling around, while two in-town riders going head to head were fed with every available job, simply to settle a bet on who could do most in a day. And nobody cared, because we were all on wages. Everyone else would simply spend more time larking around at base, or sitting in Shoe Lane cafe, getting regular updates on the docket count from new arrivals. Without any doubt our natural exuberance, insanity and spirit of competition earned more for Mercury than any bonus or incentive scheme they ever came up with.

I remember being pulled at work by a half-pissed TLB (the that time head honcho at Mercury) over a bill they'd received for graffiti in a posh Regent Street lift.

"Can you explain why "Dave 623" was written on the wall of the lifts in *Ciros?*"

"Dunno? Perhaps one of the secretaries has got the hots for me."

"This is serious. There was loads of graffiti and I've received a bill for over £200. Don't you think scrawling on walls is a bit childish?"

"Well Tony, when you put it that way... But then again, I'd hardly be working here if I was all grown up would I?"

I smiled sweetly and left, while he fumbled for an answer; but there wasn't one really. By the Winter of 1979, Mercury provided me with a bike, Helly Hensens and a Griffin Clubman – all in bright orange; they paid for all my fuel and maintenance – and paid me £85 a week + overtime (+ a bottle of Vat 69 by way of a Christmas bonus). Which was a good wage, especially when you consider that the three-bedroom flat I shared with two other couriers cost £21 per week – between us – and beer was around 50p a pint. But just to put that in perspective, in the last full working week before Christmas 1979, I earned the company over £1,000!

I can't speak for anyone else, but I certainly wasn't there for the money. I was there because it was better than working and we were having it large! My relationship with Mercury was entirely symbiotic. I might have earned them a disproportionate amount of money, but the two and a bit years I spent there provided me with some of the most vital experiences – and by extension – memories of my life.

And it still makes me grin when I'm reminded of them. That's *WHY* I went to the reunion. The past was bright... the past was orange!

Be careful out there
Caring Sharing Dave

P.S. Extra special credit for this month's title. I decided on it on the 14th March – almost a fortnight before Ian Dury's tragic death – because the song, which first charted on August 4th 1979, summed up my feelings at that time. Ian was a first rate geezer and possibly the greatest ever people's poet; he'll be sorely missed. Cheers Ian.

Fatal Attraction
TRD issue 36 – August 2000

One hundred and eighteen Russian submariners died at the bottom of the Barents Sea, victims of the fiscally frozen peace that followed the Cold War. Fortunately the grim reality of the dreadful drawn-out deaths of the crew members that were unlucky enough to survive the original torpedo explosions, were buried under a mountain of Royal Family fluff.

At the beginning of the month the nation celebrated the fact that the hundred-year-old Queen Mum, was still able to perform the Royal Wave (although 'palace insiders' admitted that she struggled with the Mexican variety). Interestingly none of the reports mentioned whether or not she received a telegram from her daughter. A fortnight later it was announced – with great pride – that Prince William (with maybe just a teeny bit of help) had managed to gain enough mediocre A levels to gain access to St Andrews – which was of course of crucial importance because attending a good university will undoubtedly do wonders for his future job prospects.

Fatal Attraction

The original working title for this month's offering was: "Women... D'oh!" However I decided that while the Homer reference (that's Simpson, not the Greek geezer) gave a clue to the subject matter, it wasn't quite right. But a recent near miss caused me to pause and contemplate the many dangers just waiting for the opportunity to teach any of us a painful lesson, so I do want to discuss women and accidents.

I'd screeched to a full-on emergency stop, narrowly avoiding a costly collision with an S-class Mercedes. The driver, a woman of around fifty with the steely glint of an '84 Thatcher, turned her head slightly in my direction, before tilting her nose disdainfully and flooring the V8. As I clunked my bike back into neutral and kicked it back to life, I couldn't help reflecting that the overwhelming majority of the accidents and near misses I'd been involved in over the years could be directly attributed to women.

I am not however, suggesting for a moment that women have been responsible whenever danger has loomed, far from it. All I'm saying is that they have often been central to the overall drama. So much so, that it would be unwise to ignore such a potentially lethal factor, when you're performing the unconscious risk assessment that's an integral part of survival on the road.

There are two sorts of danger out there. There are the kinds that are imposed on you by third parties or physical factors; and there's the other kind, the stuff that's your fault. The former are much easier to deal with, because they're constants that wise riders always keep in mind. White van man, school run battleships, drivers arguing on their mobile phones... the list goes on and on and on. It's the same with the physical bits: diesel slicks, pot holes, manhole covers; you can even bung in horse shit and, one I encountered personally, mint sauce slicks if you like. The reality is you expect the unexpected and as long as you're on the ball, you're safe.

But what happens when you're distracted? This brings me to the second danger, the Enemy Within. OK, so when the Tories coined the phrase they were referring to the miners; but what they were talking about was an enemy that could seriously fuck them up. Which, if you think what a little internal sabotage can achieve on a motorbike, is about the same thing. Of course unless you're actually psychotic you're unlikely to try to fuck yourself up, but it's funny how things turn out. A moment's distraction at the wrong time and you can suddenly find yourself in the world of special parking privileges, or even discover that your life insurance has matured.

Which brings me back to women. The battleaxe in the Mercedes had every right to look down her nose at me. Aside from the fact that merely riding a bike probably put me somewhere a few rungs beneath her contempt, I'd also shot straight across a give way line without even registering it. No, it wasn't her who reminded me of the treacherous plot by womankind to get me, she was incidental. It was the redhead's fault.

Actually that's not fair either. She may have been aware of how beautiful she was (although she'd have had to have been pretty daft to have missed it!); but, as she crossed the street between two grey blocks, she couldn't have known that the sun, as it blazed through her hair would create a copper halo that seared my brain, scorching any thought of Roadcraft from my mind. If she hadn't stepped into the shadows when she did, I've no doubt I'd have gained intimate personal experience of Benz's legendary build quality.

How would I have explained it away to my friends and family (assuming I was lucky enough to retain the ability to communicate)? I decided that I'd have called it a glitch. Glitches cause all sorts of disasters. A dodgy O-ring turned the tenth Challenger mission into a dramatic fireworks display. A mechanic forgets to bolt your callipers back to your forks... oops! Or the bolts aren't checked properly on an 80mph bend on a rail track... D'oh.

The trouble with these examples is that they're all external. Someone else screws up and the person on the receiving end cops it. The situation I'm describing is something completely different. My situation wasn't a glitch – "a sudden irregularity or malfunction" – but it was very nearly a GLITCH. A Gonad Led Intelligence Takeover & Consequential Horror.

I've never been sure about the idea that the average man thinks about sex every six seconds; I can't see it personally, not consciously. However I do believe there's a department somewhere in his brain that does nothing but. It's like an all-male office, where Darren the lech sits at the window all day going: "Cor look at that! I wouldn't mind getting its heels behind its ears... Check the tits on that Doris! I'd give it one... What about the arse on that? You could park a Goldwing up her Khyber..." It's there all the time, a background buzz, annoying, but tolerated because when Darren yells "Worrr!!" in a certain tone, everyone drops whatever they're doing and rushes to the window to press their noses against the glass.

And that's how I think it works in our heads at a *Numbskulls* level. Darren is obviously a gonadotrophin and it's his job to keep his eyes skinned for possible sperm banks. While you're riding along he's going, "Blonde left. Brunette right. Low top by the lights. Short skirt on the horizon." And most of the time the rest of your functions stay on task and concentrate on the job in hand (i.e. tearing between two rows of traffic, skimming past mirrors, and weaving past wobblers on their mobiles). Then all of a sudden Darren goes "Worrr!!" and that's it. In a fraction of a millisecond your brain is full of the boys from your bollocks. They wrench your eyes in the direction that Darren's pointing, just in time for all the lads in the hard-pressed riding department to look up and see the white silk blouse billow once again, exposing a perfectly formed honeyed orb tipped by the most... And that's about when you whack the Ikea package that's sticking out the back window of a Cinquecento, high-side it and bounce towards the bull bars of an oncoming Vitara.

It's obvious that if you're not looking at the road, it's pot luck what happens next. I've been there enough times, particularly in my earlier years, to know just how lucky I've been not to have met any excessively sharp or aggressively immovable objects in my various shunts and slides. On average, I've probably come off with little more than roadrash, the occasional ruined pair of best jeans and a bill for thirty or so quid for indicators and levers from a breaker's.

For me, the greatest boon of working on the fleet at Mercury was that you didn't even have to pay to get your bike fixed; which must have saved me a fortune in my first summer as a courier. As an in-town rider, I rode from the West End to the City and back again, all day every day. And yes I got distracted, I admit it, constantly, beautifully and often memorably, but also rather too regularly, painfully. One momentous morning, early in June 1979, I managed to dump my company bike twice within the space of a couple of hundred yards and little more than five minutes – and both spills were classic GLITCHes.

The first was around 9:45am and what was most impressive about that one was that I was stationary when it happened. I was on the sunny side of Harley Street, about twenty yards from the lights at Cavendish Square, waiting to pick up a regular ten o'clock booking at a clinic opposite. It was a glorious morning. My GT250 was on the centre-stand, and I was reclined across it in a t-shirt, with my shoulders on the topbox and my feet resting on the clocks inside the handlebar fairing. I was half-reading a copy of *Bike*, but mainly checking out the steady stream of lightly dressed women. I'd arranged the right mirror to make sure I didn't miss anyone behind me; and sure enough a blonde and a redhead, both around 18 or 19, appeared in the reflected distance. They were a picture of summer beauty; skimpily dressed, they leant on each other as they walked arm in arm, chatting and laughing. I waited until I thought they were right alongside and turned casually to show them my teeth. Sadly they weren't quite as close as I'd thought and as I turned to check my blindspot the bike toppled. I tried to extricate my boots from the fairing without success, so I went down with my ship and we tumbled in a heap at their feet. They laughed some more as they skipped round me and the redhead gave me a little finger wiggling wave as they crossed the road to walk through the gardens. Not a total loss then.

I'd no sooner sorted the bike out and settled down for another ten minutes bask, when yet another vision of loveliness – wearing a calf length dress of fine white Indian cheesecloth – drifted across the lights and disappeared past the corner heading down Wigmore Street. At the same moment the lights ahead of me turned green and it occurred to Darren and the bollock boys (who more or less had the run of things while I was standing by) that if I tore round the block real quick, I could get another look at her with the sun behind her. I kicked the Suzuki into life, rocked it off the stand and the rear wheel hit the road spinning. I sped around the square, along Henrietta Place, scraped my pannier into Wimpole Street, straightening momentarily before throwing it over again as I screamed into Wigmore Street on a very late amber. And there she was, still ten yards from the junction.

You've got to give it to Daz and the boys, they were spot on. Viewed from the West, backlit by the stark morning sunlight, she was a mindblowing naked silhouette. There wasn't a single brain cell who didn't have his nose pressed against my optical nerve; which, as it turned out, meant there was no bugger riding the bike, and accounts for why it just kept on leaning until it broke away and scraped across the road to clatter into the gutter. I picked myself up and my bare right arm had a long black and red smear from the elbow to the wrist, while the mess on the palms of my hands dissuaded me from trying to lead the excited onlookers in a spontaneous round of applause for what was, when all's said and done, a pretty spectacular bit of street entertainment.

The vision stopped alongside me and although she was clearly oblivious to any culpability on her part, she looked terribly concerned. She was another *Duracell* (yeah, of course I know there's a pattern) sporting a short carrot-coloured crop. When she opened her full-lipped mouth to speak I thought, "What the hell if my limbs smart and I've got yet another new pair of Levis with holes in the knee, I could be on a result here." But before she could speak, two lovely old dears swung to my rescue offering me tissues, sympathy, and sage words of advice against dashing around on motorbikes. The vision, seeing I was already well cared for, wrinkled her nose and twinkled her green eyes at me, before turning away and walking out of my life, leaving me with the girls explaining that they were up from Guildford for a recital at the Wigmore Hall. I firmly, but somewhat belatedly bolted the barn door, by putting my jacket and gloves on top of my wounds, made my apologies to the Surrey W.I. and shot off for the ten o'clock pick up.

These were just a couple of situations out of a thousand. Others included various Marilyn Monroe scenes above underground vents; stocking tops crossing Cheapside; even topless sunbathers in the central reservation on Park Lane! And if I was moving when they happened, my survival was likely to involve an infinitely higher ratio of luck to judgment than would normally be desirable.

I realise that, while some of you will share my fatal attraction, there'll be others who simply don't relate to any of this. If it's just a question of gender or sexual orientation, you can substitute diaphanous dresses for overfilled cycle shorts, bare-arsed chaps in chaps, or anything else that rings your bell. For a few of you it may be Ferrari Dinos, speckled throat-warblers or rare Routemaster buses, but most of us with a pulse have an Achilles heel.

So how do you avoid, or at least lower, the risk factors in these situations? I'm afraid I can only talk authoritatively about GLITCHes from a male perspective; and the best advice I can offer is to get old! Your hormones eventually get too knackered to rush to your brain in the sort of numbers they used to, so there's a better chance of maintaining at least one eye on the road. But for someone twenty-two, who's struggling to make twenty-three, I realise that's not a lot of help. So for the younger audience I'd point you to the advice given to Ted in *Something About Mary*: "Never go on a date with a loaded gun!" OK, you're not going out on a date, but the principle's the same and you've got to do something to stop them swarming across your brain and fucking you up (and don't forget Ted ended up with Cameron Diaz!).

If you're reading this in sunshine beware! You know how dangerous it's going to be out there: simply acres and acres of lightly-draped flesh, in all its wonderful variety. So give yourself an edge. Pop into a posh office block now, the kind where they have nice accessible marble and gold bogs, and empty that gun. Regular pre-emptive strikes against the enemy within may be the best shot you've got at surviving until the comparative safety of the ice and snow of yet another Winter.

Be extra careful out there when the sun shines
Carin' Sharin'

PS: If anyone has been offended by this piece, please allow me to apologise – I set out to write a serious article on the importance of good communication with your controller. Unfortunately Darren decided that was a load of old bollocks and called the boys up for support; who then ran around my brain chanting "We want crumpet!" until I caved in – sorry.

You can take the M Road...
TRD issue 38 – October 2000

Coming barely a year after the horrendous Paddington train crash that left 31 people dead, the October 17th derailment at Hatfield killed another four passengers (all of whom were in the restaurant car) and when it was revealed that the tragedy was caused by poorly maintained track, it prompted urgent calls for charges of corporate manslaughter to be brought against executives at Railtrack and Balfour Beatty. However, although substantial fines were handed down against both firms almost five years later, unsurprisingly no managers or directors of either company did any porridge.

You can take the M Road...

My car pulled away with arms waving from every window, plus the sunroof. Fortunately it wasn't a bunch of teenage TWOC merchants taking the piss, it was just the family heading off on summer holiday. My partner Becky was driving, while my four kids filled the other seats. I'd told her to go the way she knew best: down to Chelsea Bridge, round the Embankment, A4, M4, bosh bosh bosh, bridge, Wales! Not complicated, none of our usual last minute arguments, just a quick round of kisses and they'd gone.

And suddenly I was alone; sitting on my front doorstep, smoking, while I moved my head to a different space. I wasn't on any Cinderella trip, nor was I planning to make *Home Alone 7*; the plain fact is, when it comes to long journeys there simply isn't enough room for everyone in the car. I was going to join them, I was just taking a little time to drop out and tune in before I began my solo mission.

I'm still enough of a despatch rider to know the quickest route from SE19 to Dyfed, especially in a fully laden Citroën ZX; but I was going on my SRX6 and while the M4 has never been my idea of biker's heaven, on a 16 year old single with 53,000 kilometres on the clock, it would be a fucking eternity in purgatory. Nope, even though me and the family were heading for the same spot, we were on two completely different trips. If the M Snore had been the only route, I'd probably have settled for a cramped kip on a coach; but just as other despatch companies, mobile networks and ISPs are available, so are other roads West.

Any of you who've read *Zen & the Art of Motorcycle Maintenance* (even the majority who gave up when it started "getting weird") will be familiar with the concept that when making a journey on a motorcycle, the bit between A & B is more significant than actually reaching your destination. Now I know this doesn't hold up so well when you're working. That the average controller, if you tell him to be more Zen, that the trip's the important bit and he shouldn't get so hung up on all that "arriving" shit, is likely to get a bit teed off especially if you've just delivered Herbert Smith's Colnbrook half an hour after the last flight. But when you're on your own time it's a whole different story – the choice is yours. Forget about work, even David Beckham would get pissed off playing football from 9 till 7 every day, come rain or shine; cast your mind back to biking in its purest, most sublime form, when the journey really was the only point and the destination an incidental, as often as not decided by the fact that it was at the end of a particularly nice stretch of road.

OK on this occasion the finish line was preordained, but the choice of route was all mine. I pulled away from the Palace (that's Crystal, not my hutch) in the sort of sunshine that made me glad all over I hadn't bottled out when my half-arsed plans failed to arrange themselves. I'd kind of hoped that as this was my twenty-fifth summer riding a motorcycle, I might have scrounged something a bit sexier than my trusty oil-soaked Yam – something befitting a silver anniversary. But unfortunately I got caught out, forgetting that August follows on so close behind July and never quite got my shit together. As a consequence my work-and-back plodder never got the service it was overdue for either. So on the morning I was setting off on a thousand kilometre round trip, I treated it to a tyre pressure check, chain tighten & lube, and (as if in direct contradiction to the pool that always appears around it) topped up the comparatively fresh oil with a tiny amount of Motul – and that was it. Given the vintage of my bike and my 'maintenance regime', it was about the equivalent of me training for a marathon by walking up to the shops to buy my fags, instead of riding like I normally do.

However, in spite of good reasons to question the 600's ability to maintain its mechanical integrity (i.e. not fall apart in any one of the many areas it would have every right to give up the ghost in), I rode away feeling at peace with the universe. In the balmy sunshine everything felt absolutely fine and groovy – almost too good to be true – and the blast to the Westway was as swift and slick as you'd expect from a bike and rider both on home ground.

The Kamikaze pedestrians in Brixton provided the usual lively sport and MI6 got a great view of the oiliest bit of my bike (plus a throaty raspberry, courtesy of my lovely Supertrapp exhaust) as I swept onto Vauxhall Bridge. At Hyde Park Corner, Marble Arch and Lancaster Gate, I resisted the temptation to shout "Oy! Get out of my city!" to all the weekend drivers up from the sticks; although it was a laugh scaring the manure out of them, as I roared past while they circulated as if they were on tractors.

It was all fun and gently playing with the traffic, right the way to somewhere around Uxbridge. Once past there the steady 75mph cruising speed I was maintaining (a figure I'd negotiated with my bike, when it bravely agreed to attempt the journey) meant I seemed to spend a lot of time looking back at the same old faces in Volvo 440s, Maestros, and Skodas. There was little on the M40 to keep me interested, but I'd allowed for that little bit of tedium. After all there was no point in being masochistic and doing High Wycombe and all the other crap towns on the old A40 just to make a point. If by the time I reached the Irish Sea, the worst I'd had to put up with was a bit of drudgery with the herd between the M25 and Oxford, I'd be on a result.

The moment I rolled off the M40 at Oxford, the bike seemed tighter and more urgent, and although it's dual carriageway right the way in and around the ring road, the roundabouts helped to blow away any motorway fuzziness long before I hit the old A40 proper. From the edge of the city on down towards Gloucester, with the exception of the odd bit of by-pass, the road is very much as it has been since long before the first bridge was built to allow a more direct route between the Capital and South Wales. I travelled it regularly in the fifties & sixties with my family (back when bench seats meant you could get two adults and a shit load of kids in a car).

It was on one of our holidays in Swansea that I had my first bike ride, aged ten, on the back of my eighteen-year-old Uncle Paul's cafe racer. I still have a child's eye memory, of roaring up and around the hills and hairpins of

Townhill. It was along the A40 that he and his friends used to thunder on Gold Stars, Triumph 110s, Venoms, Dominator 99s, or any one of another dozen or so (British) bikes and hybrids, that were up for a serious 200 mile blast. I sent Paul an e-mail, asking what sort of times they expected on the Swansea to London run and got this back:

"Individual times from the bottom of Wind Street, to the Ace cafe on the North Circular close to Hanger lane were always bandied about and I personally completed that run two-up on several occasions, with the time of two and a half hours always being the decent time to match. This always discounted a stop at the transport cafe in Gloucester which was sorely needed given the rough rides of that day. I'm talking here of 1965-ish (on the bikes listed above). Hard ride with one half-hour break. 3 hours, done by many, bettered by few..."

Funny when you think that now, a cafe racer is normally a bike which is mass-produced in Japan, tarted-up with plastic and sold to wannabe racers – who then use it to tear from KFC to the McDonald's drive-through and back again. Thirty-five years ago it was very much an individual machine, stripped down, tuned up, and usually drilled and wired to stop it shaking itself apart. Cafe racing was exactly what they were doing then and is therefore the perfect example of the ride as the whole point. Paul and the other ton-up boys (and girls), didn't race to the Ace because it served the best all day breakfast within a 200 mile radius; they did it because it lay at the other end of a testing ride (By the way, anyone who's unimpressed with the times quoted, ought to bear in my mind that although there wasn't the traffic then, by extension, there weren't any by-passes! So they had to go through Cardiff, Gloucester, Oxford, High Wycombe and a host of smaller towns and villages on the A40 and 48 en route to their egg, bacon, bubble and beans).

However on my trip, I was more interested in sharing their feeling of freedom than taking a tilt at any licence-shredding, pre-national speed limit, records. The 75mph which had been such a drone on the motorway, was a good pace on the pleasantly undulating A road; and a short blast to 85 or 90 was plenty to turn a trio of posing R1s into blurred history in the bar-end, as I rolled past the traffic and round the sweeping bends.

I pulled into Northleach well on reserve, and failing to find a petrol station I stopped for a Tango, a fag, and a Boost before heading back to the A40. But I didn't even make the quarter mile back to the main road before the bike, going uphill on full throttle, coughed twice and trickled to a halt. As I looked up and down the road pathetically a Land Rover pulled out of the dairy farm opposite, and when I shouted across to the driver he told me the closest petrol was a bit less than a mile back down the hill and up over the other side. What had been a glorious sunny day looked like turning into its downside: a long sweaty push.

Fortunately the farmer turned out to be a genuine "milkman of human kindness", because as I took off my lid and started to push, he spotted me in his mirror and did a three-pointer. He apologised, saying he hadn't realised I was already dry and told me to wait there for a moment. I wasn't desperately disappointed at not having to push the bike, so I lit another fag and waited.

He was back from his farmyard with a can before I'd finished it and I gratefully tipped in the 5 quid's worth of unleaded he informed was inside. It was no surprise when he said he rode a bike and as I gratefully handed over a fiver and waved him off, I couldn't help reflecting that considering I was trying to be very Zen about this journey, I had to be sitting on some seriously good karma. I'd gone from a severely burst bubble (i.e. the prospect of pushing my bike uphill under the hottest sun I'd felt all summer) to back on the road rescued, in less time than it takes to suck a Silk Cut down to the butt.

After topping the bike up, I stayed on the A40 right through to Abergavenny and although it was dual carriageway all the way from Ross-on-Wye, it had the occasional roundabout and was never tedious with Monmouthshire as a backdrop. In Abergavenny I considered stopping at the cafe by the river, where there were thirty or forty bikes fanned around the car park; but I'd have felt like I'd turned up at a white tie and tails do in Bermudas and sandals. Someone must have slaughtered lots of very shiny multicoloured cows because everyone, bar none, seemed to be wearing coordinated leathers, complete with knee sliders. I wasn't unduly ashamed of my jeans, lace up copy Caterpillars, black leather jacket and cheap black crash hat, but I didn't want to embarrass my trusty bike by exposing it to all that garish plastic.

Instead I chose the Abergavenny pizza, burger, kebab, fish & chips, Indian and Chinese take-away. I went for the burger and took it away to sit on the bike outside. There I had a great chat with the old guy whose wife cooked everything inside. "There's lovely the A40 is on a bike like that." he reassured me, while I dropped tomato and mayonnaise onto the flies that spattered the front of my jacket. When I was leaving, he told me to make sure I checked out an obelisk, which I'd find alongside the road just before Llandovery. It was erected in 18 something or the other and commemorates a mail coach crash where around a dozen people died. I promised to keep an eye out and reverberated out of town.

Of course he was right about the road, but then I knew that. The Romans thought they were real clever bastards, what with their baths and straight roads that go on forever; but what good are either of them to a biker? The Welsh have got it better sussed. They looked at the mountains and said, sod knocking that lot down, let's follow the rivers and chip a bit off the edge. A few years ago the Chief Inspector of some County in Mid Cymru was complaining in the press about bikers coming to Wales and treating it like a racetrack. To which my friend Mark replied: "Serves them right for having such lovely roads and so much breathtaking fucking scenery running alongside them."

I pulled into Brecon to fill up, exhilarated by the ride but had a nasty start when I saw an excessive number of yellow jackets and blue pointy hats at the edge of town. It turned out they were there for the Jazz Festival rather than any sweep against bikers; but that didn't stop me from freaking a bit when I got caught in a diversion and went on a long Stephen King type loop, which, after two or three miles, brought me back to ride noisily past them again. I got it right second time 'round and headed off in a light drizzle that looked like it might pass. By the time I reached the monument I'd been advised to check out, it seemed like a good time to put my waterproofs on. I read an inscription warning against the dangers of insobriety while driving and reached in my pocket for a smoke… Which was when I noticed the gap where my wallet should have been.

I'd used it in the petrol station, I remembered carrying it into the bog with my gloves… Shit! I scrubbed round the waterproofs, kicked the bike back to life and shot off back in the direction I'd just come from. The rain got heavier and I passed a number of bikes with a lot more rubber, but clearly less sense of urgency. I slowed down as I pulled into Brecon because the police had already had two opportunities to make a fuss about my exhaust and it seemed silly to push my luck. I'd ridden all the way back with all thoughts of happy hippy karma dissolving in the rain, but half a dozen words with the young guy behind the counter saw me beaming all over my face, not even pissed off that it required another £4.10 to restore the tank to where it had been three quarters of an hour earlier.

There was no point in putting my waterproofs on by then, my nuts were as wet as they were going to get and I didn't see much benefit in sealing everything in plastic. I waved to the obelisk as I passed it and waved goodbye to the A40 shortly after, when I headed up the A482 towards Lampeter. As I followed the river route, I couldn't help reflecting that if I hadn't listened to the guy in Abergavenny, I'd have been miles further, perhaps at my destination, before I discovered my cock-up. The thought of that kept me buoyed as the sun, which had been around throughout the rain, finally outran me.

When my headlight fell off, I was well and truly in the dark. One minute I was riding along with rain plopping through the canopy of trees and the river on my left; the next, there were a serious set of chevrons ahead and a road narrows sign, indicating I needed to peel off a lot of speed fast to swing over a humpback bridge and switch banks. I compressed the forks, hit a few bumps and my headlight, minus retaining bolts, leapt off its casing and dangled like a glow worm near the front wheel. Inwardly I screamed "Shiiit!!!" but I'd been riding at such a pitch due to the conditions, I managed to stop without dumping it or shearing off the cables that provided my lifeline.

I'd hit a rhythm that had allowed me to ignore the seeping dampness, and the night ride on unfamiliar wet roads had become perversely enjoyable. So I hooked the light back on at the top and pushed it back into place. With nothing to secure it, I decided I'd keep it on by the power of positive thought. I didn't do too bad either. After it had fallen off a second time, I realised it gave a wobbling warning flicker before it dived for the floor; and three or four stops to push it back into place saw me in Fishguard asking directions from a quartet of young lovelies outside a pub. They stood there in their teeny dresses, oblivious to the steady rain, and directed me to my journey's end with their gorgeous Cerys Matthews accents.

Ten minutes later I was dripping at my destination – almost against the odds, but never against the grain. I could have taken the motorway and saved myself a load of time, but I've never understood that concept. Where do you keep the time you've saved? And when do you get to use it? Half a day spent stimulating all your senses, meeting people and following the course of ancient roads and even older rivers on a willing bike is like Alka-seltzer for the soul! Why would anyone want to foreshorten the experience? People pay good money on drugs to get to that sort of place. Three hours of mind numbing M4 is an eighth of a day pissed away, with absolutely nothing to show for it. Why waste any of your life? You never know when the odd eighth could make all the difference.

Nah, when it comes to a trip on a bike: You can take the M road; I'll take the Zen road.

Be careful out there - take it karma!
Carin' Sharin'

Precious Children
TRD issue 39 – November 2000

It was November 2000 when George W Bush, aided and abetted by his brother Jeb – the governor of Florida – and Fox News, pulled off the great US presidential election rip-off that landed him in the White House and the ordinary American people in the middle of the biggest shit-storm they'd ever seen – and eight years down the line, the series of grim consequences and repercussions they've been suffering, have continued to mount on a daily, weekly and monthly basis.

Meanwhile back in the UK, I wrote Precious Children in response to an article in issue 37 by regular TRD contributor "Wulf", whose experiences in Kuala Lumpa left him questioning the wisdom of carrying children on motorcycles. He finished his piece with the following:

"I'm not saying what you should do. I'm only saying that maybe we should all take some time to think calmly and clearly exactly who we are doing it for in the first place. It's raw risk on a third-world scale – with a payoff that no amount of compensation or being faultless will touch if the coin lands face-down. Are you ready for that? I found myself left with one last unpleasant question: did I want to give my child the gift of biking or my biking the gift of my child?

Think about it next time you take your child out on the road with you."

Precious Children

In September, Wulf was in "dad" mode. As a father, the sights he'd seen in Malaysia forced him to seriously reconsider the wisdom of carrying his cubs on his motorcycle. In particular, seeing a man precariously balancing the life of a sleeping baby on the petrol tank of his moped forced him to confront the naked peril you expose your child to when you allow (or worse still, encourage) it to ride on your pillion. Not only did he question the "raw risk on a third world scale", but he also had to contend with the worrying possibility that he could end up giving his biking the gift of his child. However, having flagged a serious quandary he didn't offer much by way of answers, guidance or insight before signing off with the suggestion that the reader "think about it".

Personally I didn't need to give it a great deal of thought; due to the age of my children it was ground I'd covered long ago. My 9, 15 and 17 year-olds have all been out on the road on my various bikes; and my 4 year-old is just waiting until I'm sure he's got both the height and the savvy to keep his feet firmly placed on the pegs before be joins them; until then he's had the occasional trip up and down the private cul-de-sac that adjoins our road, since he was three. But does that make me a terrible dad? Does it mean that I don't really think or care enough? That I'm being cavalier with my children's lives?

Should parents allow their children to be exposed to the potentially horrific dangers of biking? It's an important question; because if not, then surely you have to take it to its logical conclusion and attempt to ban them from all the hazards you've encountered, from drugs to unprotected sex, even though you got to make your own choices and survived. It's a dilemma which has troubled parents for generations; and one which will almost certainly continue to cause arguments and divisions, way beyond a point in the future when allowing your child to take any risk will constitute a criminal offence.

I arrived at the basis of my own decision some years ago, so when I read what the big bad one had to say, I thought I'd better go back over the ground with a couple of other biking parents. With nine saucepans between us, Paul (3), Dave (2) and me (4), would seem to constitute a pretty reasonable cross-section. We all have at least one child of each sex and each of them (with the exception of my youngest) has, aside from riding pillion, ridden motocross bikes themselves.

I took the photo at the top in August '97 at Tommy's farm in Wales. It shows Paul and Dave with just about the entire fruit of our loins mounted on bikes like lambs prepared for the slaughter. Are we all such bad parents? A week or so ago, when we had what is nowadays a rare night where we were all together, I decided I'd check their views before I wrote this. I thought it might be useful to sound out their reasoning, as we'd all arrived at our own conclusions separately and without any consultation. But I got the kind of responses I should have known to expect after twenty odd years. Paul made some quip about kids having as much right to die having fun as we have; while Dave shrugged, tipped his head to one side and inquired why I was asking him stupid questions that it would take us hours to disappear up our arses about, when all three of us already knew the answer. However, both of them, in their own sweet way, and without resorting to any protracted ethical or moral arguments, reminded me that I had thought it through and that, given my views on life – and death – had arrived at the only possible conclusion.

In the small hours after my third child was born, I arrived home elated, plonked myself in front of the TV and a programme came on about R.D.

Laing: pre-eminent psychologist, occasional acid head, 60s liberal thinker and all round very interesting fella. At one point his face filled the screen and he smiled at me wryly before stating in an alcohol-slurred voice that: "Life is a sexually transmitted disease, with a 100% mortality rate". Bang! Have another toke and ponder that one! Which I did. A couple of miles away in King's College Hospital, Nick, who was hours old, was sleeping while his mother lay awake, watching him in wonder. Meanwhile I was in Brixton with a pissed jock telling me my boy's meter was already running. The best bit was that I couldn't argue with a word he said. Obviously his choice of words was designed to cut through all the bullshit and hearts and flowers, to remind the viewer of the only absolute certainty in life. He wasn't being nasty. He was simply saying not to waste your life worrying about dying, because it's the one thing you can rely on so you may as well get on with living. Roddy Frame, a fellow Scot, put it a lot more gently when he said: "Life's a one-take movie..." but the principle's the same.

Of course I'm aware my kids are going to die, but I'm not banking on seeing it. With the sort of medical advances they'll witness, unless anything should happen to precipitate the process they might even double the 'three score years and ten' the bible offers as a standard. Between now and then though, there are a lot of things that could happen; so if you're really serious about longevity, you simply can't afford to take risks. But where do you draw the line?

For some people, getting out of bed is too risky. You only have to look at Howard Hughes to see the world turned upside down. One of the richest men on the planet and pretty damn clever with it, he'd had a whole heap of fun in his youth. So what did he do in the end? Did he have a Scrooge-like moment of revelation and give his enormous wealth to the needy of the world? Did he turn into a sad old up-market prototype for pathetic rakes like Peter Stringfellow and wheel through an ever-younger line up of lovelies? Did he bollocks! What he did was lock himself away and walk around in pyjamas with tissue boxes on his feet, while he obsessed about germs and all the other things just queuing up to get him. Obviously he'd lost the plot, but the dangers were clearly all too real for him and his fear of them consumed his life.

So how do you assess a risk objectively? The truth is you can't, particularly if it involves your child. Objectivity requires the kind of distance and detachment you get from insurance companies and the legal system, not parents. The former work out the odds and the latter tell you what you can and cannot do; but as they've both become nasty scabs as a result of the drippy-dick relationship with the good ol' US of A that Wulf alluded to, it would hardly seem appropriate to trust them to decide what's best for your own flesh and blood.

So in the end it all comes back to you. You can ask yourself *Daily Mail* questions like: Which would do your child most harm, dying as a result of a bike accident, or never going on one in the first place? You don't need to go all the way to Kuala Lumpur to find the answer. But the choice isn't that stark. For the question to mean anything it needs to examine all the possible outcomes. You'd also need to weigh the likelihood of a perfect trip, that will sparkle in your child's memory for the rest of its life against keeping it in a windowless nuclear bunker to protect it from all evils. Any risk assessment needs to take a holistic view of the entire spectrum. At one end lies an awful death; but at the other lies the greater tragedy of an awful life.

The question the lupine one was really asking was, are you prepared for the kind of worst-case scenario that a bike is more than able to provide – the gruesome death of your child. But before you ask that question, you have to ask a more fundamental one: Are you prepared for the death of your child? I think the answer, for any parent who hasn't actually been forced to confront it, has to be 'No'. Many worry about it, some fixate on it, but I don't believe any parent who hasn't had to go there could possibly begin to imagine how it would feel, much less want to.

I consider myself quite staunch when it comes to looking reality straight in the eye, but I have never in my worst nightmare even attempted to torture my mind with having to deal with that particular reality. Why should I? I've spent the last seventeen years doing the best I know how to make sure I never have to. I replace batteries in smoke detectors, check their seat belts are done up properly, make sure they eat their veg and all the other sensible stuff. Between times, I warn them what's most likely to kill or seriously fuck them up.

In a nutshell, I do what I can, but there's danger everywhere, even in the most innocent or mundane situation. If Wulf's metaphorical coin does its fatal flip, it doesn't matter where your child is, your life will never be the same.

My children have all had great experiences on bikes, without anything remotely resembling serious danger so much as waving to us as we went past.

Of course that doesn't mean it will always be the case, but the odds don't increase with each journey; they're always about the same or go down as you get older and wiser. Fate isn't a fifty-fifty toss of a coin, it's a lottery; and millions of people fail to come up on the lottery every single week.

I wouldn't dare to tell anybody else what to do with their babies, because I can only truly be responsible for mine. But if I'd had any nagging doubts they'd have evaporated on Nick's eighth birthday, a couple of Aprils ago. My SRX had been off the road for six months and as I'd finished it just the day before, I'd agreed that we'd go to school on it as a birthday treat. As we pulled up by the gate with a roar, half his schoolmates looked up from the playground below; and as he removed his helmet and waved to them, even his ears were glowing. I watched him walk proudly down the stairs carrying his lid into a small crowd; and as I rode off, I could still hear his voice buzzing with excitement and pride as he spoke to his *bredren*: "Yeah, it's my dad's. He's just rebuilt it. I used to go on it all the time. I've even ridden an 80cc motocrosser myself when I was only six..."

Your duty to your children extends beyond merely keeping them safe. Of course you want them to outlive you; but never forget just how important you are to them. You're meant to stick around to help them with the tricky bits, to teach them how to enjoy themselves safely by example and to help provide them with the memorable bits until they're old enough and independent enough to create their own. It's no good copping out of the whole worry of parenthood by forgetting just how fragile your own life is.

A few years ago, there was a little girl on the back of Total fuel tankers, who always made me think of my Sam. So when she prayed "Please drive carefully daddy", I'd consciously turn the wick up a little in my brain.

If you can't carry your child around with you at all times to remind you how enormously precious your life is to them perhaps you need to discard all your leathers, boots and body armour and stick to riding in trainers, a jock strap and an open face – that'll help you keep your child in focus. Never forget: you're all daddies, mummies, sons or daughters;

So whatsay you be careful out there?
Carin' Sharin'

Accidents Happen
TRD issue 40 – December 2000

The hot news was the heavily guarded showbiz wedding of Material Girl Madonna and mockney Lock Stock director Guy Ritchie, a few days before Christmas at an exclusive ceremony in the Scottish highlands; whilst at the other extreme of the temperature scale, the nation ground to a halt at the end of the month when a powerful cold weather front known as The Snowplough swept across the country delivering the first UK-wide snow covering in six years and temperatures as low as –13C in the parts of the Midlands.

Accidents Happen

Over the last three years, there have been innumerable words printed in these pages on the pros, cons, risks, dangers and sheer joys of despatch riding and by extension, about biking in the broader sense. There've been almost as many opinions as there've been authors, with arguments for and against just about any conceivable position. Interestingly, whilst occasionally there's been consensus, the most significant thing you learn listening to other people's opinions is that most people have established beliefs and convictions; and tend to maintain their assumed position, irrespective of the weight of any arguments or evidence to the contrary.

Let's try something we can all agree on: bikes have the potential to severely fuck you up. Anyone who disagrees with that, besides not being long for this world if they ride one, is also ignoring the basic rules of physics. A straightforward mathematical calculation can tell you exactly how much potential energy your body possesses at any given time. If you want to work out your momentum at a particular speed, it's easy, you simply multiply your mass by your velocity. Then all you have to do is factor in your deceleration time and you can work out, in p.s.i. exactly how much force you would hit a solid wall with. When you realise, that at any sort of speed you're talking about tons per square inch – and that your soft and crunchy bits constitute the only crumple zone – it brings to mind the old joke about the fly hitting your visor at 120 mph: 'What's the last thing that goes through it's mind? It's arse!'

Let that one percolate for a few moments. I'm not trying to worry anyone, I'm hardly broadcasting a secret! I established last month that I've accepted that at some time between now and the far distant future, I will die. I've looked at it, dealt with it and consequently rarely give it a thought – it certainly doesn't keep me awake nights. It's the same with the most extreme horrors bikes have to offer. Maths aside, we all have a kind of peripheral idea of the possibilities; it's just that some people choose not to confront them, so they lurk at the back of their minds and fuck with their heads. To live and ride with a clear head, it's worth considering your most drastic scenario thoroughly, so you know you've made the kind of informed choice Roger, Wulf and all the other 'advanced motoring and body armour' types bang on about.

It's fascinating hearing someone else's perception of the danger biking presents and the kind of precautions they deem essential for the level of risk involved. I'd be interested to discover how many people there are who wouldn't dream of riding a bike without leather and Kevlar in all the right places; but fantasise about little else than indulging in a little bareback sex. And if the opportunity came up with the right person, would they consider the risks or jump at the chance? I haven't checked the figures, but there's got to be more people dying annually as a consequence of unprotected sex (and that's not a reference to last month's "Life is a sexually transmitted disease..." line) than ever shrug off the coil on a bike. So I guess risk must be just another question of perception.

At home, I've been told off for my trashy analogies – apparently they lower the whole tone of my writing(!?). But sex and motorcycles both offer such extremes of pleasure, danger and pain, that I can't resist using one to illustrate a point about the other. There's something about the commonality between an activity that's a basic urge at a hormonal level and another that has its origins in a fundamental drive to procreate. If you were to take the same unblinkered view of the dangers involved in the exchange of body fluids as I'm suggesting for biking, you'd check medical pictures of dick rot; the reality of living, or dying, with AIDS, and the implications and complications of an unexpected or unwanted pregnancy. You need to think beforehand, because temptation is a powerful thing; and with sex, as with biking, you're unlikely to come to any satisfactorily sensible decisions in the headlong rush to get naked and inside or outside of someone you're hot for. And face it, the last thing you want when you're in or on the saddle enjoying a dream ride is to suddenly have pictures of decaying genitals, or thick stone walls with spikes on, flashing through your mind (unless you are actually trying to slow yourself down, that is).

It makes sense to decide what you consider a sensible level of protection in a calm calculated and considered way, so that if you suddenly find yourself in a hot situation, you can go with the flow. Naked to all risks undeniably gets you closer to the fun, but taking the minor precaution of wearing a few microns of latex – or a crash-hat, jacket, boots and gloves – hardly distances you from the action either, so there's plenty of room to strike a balance. Obviously there are those who wouldn't feel safe unless they were wearing two anal-strength condoms, a femidom and gum dams, just in case – and they probably ride like double-wrapped, armoured Michelin people. But it begs the question: what's the point? If your take on the dangers is that extreme, why not play safe? Forget about bikes and consensual jollies; buy a Volvo and drive somewhere nice for a wank.

Here's my opinion: accidents happen. I realise there are those who come from a Roadcraft/IAM perspective for whom that's blasphemy, and in my work there are plenty of Freudians who'll ask you to step outside if you even dare to suggest there's any such thing as a coincidence. In a perverse way they're both right. There may be a reason for everything, but that has nothing to do with the world we live in. No human has the information or the wherewithal to predict every factor, there are just too many. The idea of a computer that could anticipate butterfly effects and map chaos is an IT wet dream. In your world, it's more a case of London bus effects or chill factor than any of the more subtle nuances. The real miracle is that more shit doesn't happen.

I know why you lot are still alive, because you're all red hot, street-smart professional riders. But if that's the whole reason, why aren't there more dead pizza boys? We all laugh about them and by and large the jokes are true, so you'd expect them to have the life expectancy of a 1940 Hurricane pilot; but clearly, whatever justice would suggest, that isn't the case. Why do first-rate riders, who do everything by the book, die in freak circumstances? What about Sludge?

Hardly a rules man; but when he found himself having major surgery and an eighteen month vacation, it was plain bad luck. He was replacing a blown fuse on the hard shoulder, when a car with a shattered windscreen chose that spot to dive for safety. Bang. A simple case of wrong time, wrong place.

A few years ago when I hit the kind of spot that Wulf seemed to be describing in November's issue, I took advantage of my caring sharing (not) employer's staff support scheme and treated myself to the half dozen one hour therapy sessions that I was entitled to. After my last session was over, I was leaving feeling pretty pleased that in spite of my earlier misgivings, I wasn't completely useless and apparently I hadn't made a total bollocks of my life after all. So when my head man chucked in a little tossaway on the way out, it left me pondering for days. As I was walking out the door, he'd said: "But what if it was all luck?" I remember driving home thinking: 'You bastard, there I was believing I was all sorted; then you bung in a BIG question after the final whistle!'

My partner and my best friend told me once that I think too much! But I never understood what they meant. Your brain's a product of evolution, not apiece of crap manufactured by a capitalist consumer society, with designed-in obsolescence. It's the ultimate computer, the more you use it, the better it gets. So I applied my forty years of experience and knowledge to the question. Could it really all be luck? And what do we mean by luck anyway?

I came to my own conclusion after a couple of days of reflection; but a book I read a few years later summed it up in a page. The author used *Winnie the Pooh* to explain Taoism in a nice simple way for beginners. So I figure if he can screw with ancient and venerable teachings in order to point The Way, the least I can do is update it again, to bung a little candlepower into the darkness for you lot: -

Joe Cool was speaking to his *Daily Express*-reading neighbour Charlie, who remarked how lucky Joe's son was to have won that lovely new red bike in the 'spot the ball' competition. It was so much more roadworthy than his dangerous old bike. Joe, a very wise and serene man, nodded thoughtfully for a moment, before smiling enigmatically and saying: "Maybe".

A few days later, having heard that the son had wrapped the 916 round a Micra and was in hospital with a whole box of *Meccano* sticking out of his right leg, Charlie came over to commiserate, saying how terribly unlucky that was. Joe nodded thoughtfully for a moment before smiling enigmatically and saying: "Maybe".

A week later, after the tragic sinking of an Isle of Man ferry killed 127 people including nine out of twelve of the son's friends, Charlie was back. He was amazed at the son's good fortune: he'd booked when they had, six months earlier, and if he hadn't shattered his leg... A real stroke of luck! Joe nodded thoughtfully for a moment before smiling enigmatically and saying: "Maybe".

When I had my first smash (typically about a month after I bought my first bike) I lay on a hospital treatment bed, watching peroxide fizzle in my open wounds and mumbled to myself not to be so fucking pathetic. The nurse, thinking I was berating myself for wincing told me I didn't have to be brave. "Nah," I told her, "I'll cry if I need to. I just started a big What If? You see, I was going to come a different way; and IF I had, I wouldn't have been there when that car turned right... but I realised what a load of old tut that was. I had come that way. I was there. And it did hurt. IF never came into it. As my brother says: "IF your Aunt had bollocks, she'd be your Uncle."

"Exactly... and besides if I know anything, you were an accident waiting to happen," she reassured me. "Sure, if you're going to talk of ifs and buts, you're lucky you didn't go the other way; you could have met with a bejaysus of a big truck and had a rake of Consultant Surgeons looking after you now, instead of one pretty little colleen."

She was right. Lying in a hospital with both elbows, both hands, your left knee and left ankle all liberally smeared with strawberry jam, it can sometimes be difficult to spot your good fortune. But you only have to begin to imagine a full stop head-on at speed; the crushing wheels of an artic; or a catastrophic collision with a sharp piece of street furniture – any of them with or without the benefit of body armour – to be able to count your blessings.

I'd replace Joe Cool's "maybe", with a "so far, so good", but the effect's the same. Life's like a game of poker: you never know how you've done until you leave the table. After I'd thought about my BIG question, I decided that if I'd managed to get that far by a combination of luck and good judgment, I'd be a damn fool to mess with a good game plan. So in the end I guess the question each of us has got to ask ourselves is: Do you feel lucky?

Well do you, punk?

Be careful out there, but above all be lucky
Carin' Sharin'

A.C.A.B (Or are they?)
TRD issue 41 – January 2001

With a Department of Health report at one end of the month revealing that grotesque GP Harold Shipman may well have killed as many as three hundred of his patients and the deaths of over 25,000 people as a result of the Gujarat earthquake at the other, it's hardly surprising that Peter Mendelson's resignation from the cabinet after being accused of 'fixing' a passport application for Indian billionaire Srichand Hinduja, was the comparatively small news. However, it was the second time since New Labour's election in 1997 that the arch spin-doctor and close confident of Prime Minister Tony Blair had been forced to quit in disgrace.

A.C.A.B (Or are they?)

I caught a flash of orange ahead and gave my GT250 a little extra, shaving a few more percentage points off my margin of error as I rode west along Bishopsgate. I caught the other Mercury bike as we crossed London Wall, which was when the rider spotted me and stopped poodling about. We swung right, cutting straight across the flow of traffic without a pause, and screamed down Threadneedle Street like a pair of banshees on heat. As we blasted across the Bank our wheels were so close that pedestrians who'd jumped back in terror as the first bike raced past did a horrified double take, as their near-death experience came with a built-in aftershock.

The lights at Queens Street turned green just ahead of us, so we shot through the gap and past the front cars so fast that they almost stalled in shock. With a hundred yards or so of clear road ahead, we both jammed our throttles on the stops and raced to the right-hander. I was the last to brake, which gave me the perfect line to ride round the outside and take the inside line for the all-important left-hander into Cannon Street. As I tossed the GT from right to left, I caught a peripheral glimpse of something white over my right shoulder and as I whipped my head the other way, my blood ran cold as I saw one of the City's finest tucked in less than two feet behind my topbox. My speed disappeared almost as quickly as my grin, and I sensed that my day had taken a sudden turn for the worse. He whipped alongside and barked "Follow me!" in such a tone that it never occurred to me not to. A single twist of his right wrist followed by a couple of toots was all he needed to haul in the other rider and the three of us came to a halt on Ludgate Hill.

We pulled up directly opposite Old Bailey. The cop ordered my *compadre* in crimes and misdemeanours to wait by his bike, before turning on me; pen and pad in hand. He asked if I knew how long he'd been following me, which worried me just to think about it. I suggested Queen Victoria Street rather optimistically, to which he raised his eyebrows, before informing me that he'd seen me checking my A to Z at the top of Commercial Street!

Every fluid ounce of blood in my body went south. My lunatic blast from E1 to where I now stood almost within the shadow of the scales of justice tripped through my mind like a bad acid nightmare. Watching it suddenly bereft of adrenalin made me cringe, as the officer recounted his perspective (the one he'd present in court in that flat tone they do so well) chalking up my offences as he went along: reckless riding, speeding, driving without due care and attention, overtaking on a pedestrian crossing... As the list went on and on, I could just picture the appalled faces on the bench - and the Chair reaching for the black cap.

I was sick at my own stupidity. I'd started in the courier business at the beginning of November, and had spent about five months (most of them in the grindingly bitter winter conditions which had arrived on New Year's Eve) doing shit new boy work, on a series of mangled pool bikes. It had only been in the past few weeks that I'd finally become sufficiently established to get my own personal fleet bike and onto the in-town circuit where everything happened. It had all coincided beautifully with the first buds of spring; but as I stood there listening to his damning assessment of my suitability for public roads, I saw my newly-realised dream job being snatched away from me before the first heat of summer. And I had no one to blame but myself – it wasn't as if the lawman was making any of it up.

After listing everything he had on me, he offered me the opportunity to say something. He wasn't a youngster and he cranked the tension up to ten; before saying he'd got my details and if he ever stopped me in the City again – for anything – he'd bung this lot on top and have me banned forever. I was nearly sick with relief and had to fight to control a strong urge to kiss him. Instead, I decided to take his advice and off I pissed before he changed his mind.

Back in a day when a tattoo was more likely to be a rough-edged job, done with a needle and India ink (rather than designer Indian script, mis-spelt on the golden boy of English football), A.C.A.B. was a popular knuckle decoration. For anyone who's unfamiliar with this acronym, it stands for: "All Coppers Are Bastards" and echoes a cry many of us have uttered at one time or another. But is it entirely fair? Even if he were unique, my man in the City would demand that the "A" be changed to an "M" for "Most", because surely there can be no question about the legitimacy of his parents' relationship! On that occasion, even if never before or since, he was undeniably one of the good guys. He had me bang to rights – and not on any arbitrary speeding charge either but on a serious case of reckless stupidity – and for whatever reason, he decided that the greater good would be best served by scaring the shit out of me, before issuing me with a stern warning. And to this day, I have no doubt he was spot on. Gawd bless his wisdom and humanity!

Generalisations are difficult to argue with, because any evidence which counters them will invariably be dismissed as exceptions that prove the rule, before the overwhelming weight of conventional wisdom is wheeled out to back it up. Consequently, groups as diverse as police officers, white van drivers, Kosovans (and asylum seekers generally), security guards, Muslims, even women – and they're over fifty per cent of the population for fuck's sake – are regularly glossed over with brushstrokes as wide as the Westway. I hate generalisations. Not only are they lazy, but more often than not, when you actually examine them closely, they're not even true. In my humble opinion, the sum total of what "everybody else knows" is bollocks! In fact I'll take it further: simply by putting the words 'conventional' and 'wisdom' together, you provide the perfect illustration of a contradiction in terms; because in my experience the more widely a belief is held to be "fact", the less likely it is to hold up to any sort of serious scrutiny.

So what about the police? In *Homage to Catalonia* George Orwell wrote: "… But when I see an actual flesh-and-blood worker in conflict with his natural enemy, the policeman, I do not have to ask myself which side I am on." I'm with him all the way on that one; and if you find yourself in an actual battle, whether it be at Wapping, Orgreave coking plant, or somewhere in the Spanish Civil War, the people who are attacking you are usually being seriously unfriendly, so it makes sense to dehumanise them and revile the fatherless bastards wholesale. But on a day-to-day basis it's only the TSG, Armed Response Units and the various other stormtroopers of "Political Will" who seem to make it their mission to generate hate and fear.

Unless you're particularly unlucky, most of the traffic police you come across are generally only bastards in the same way referees are; and I can remember enough after work "friendly" footy matches in Hyde Park – played without a referee, in trainers with "mates" in motocross boots – to appreciate the scant protection offered by the man in black on Hackney marshes of a Sunday. Nobody wants officialdom to rain on his or her parade; and everyone knows the worst sort of bastard ref is the scumsucker who gives a decision against you or your team. Well it's the same with the police. We all know what the rules are and while it might be a bummer when you are caught, there's no point in blaming the Old Bill.

Crossing green lights on the Eastern Avenue in the wee small hours, doing a ton when you should be doing forty, the last thing you'd want to meet is a Traffic cop. Or is it? Personally, if my bike was up to it, my biggest worry would be meeting an acne factory in a GTi, which is older than he is (but still has a management chip that's more sophisticated than him) who thinks there's no point in waiting for red lights at that time of night – especially when you're out trying to impress a Doris. I'm glad the police are out there, if only because they offer some degree of protection from people like him and all the other murderers and manslaughterers lurking on the road.

I know there are loads of you out there who race everywhere all the time. Not because you're under any illusion that you'll arrive tangibly quicker, but simply because you lurve that feeling when the adrenaline kicks in like nitro. I've seen you out there wheelie-ing away from lights and scraping around corners. Even if I hadn't, I'd know you existed, because for as long as despatching on motorbikes is there as an option, there will be an inexhaustible supply of takers who want nothing more than a steady stream of excuses for a little heads-down no-nonsense mindless boogie (apologies to *Albertos YLTP*). Truth is, even wrinklies like me stray above prescribed speed limits, but nobody wants to be flagged offside.

However, the alternative to traffic regulations and enforcement wouldn't be anarchy, it would be chaos – with a small c. In spite of what "everybody else knows", anarchy isn't about disorder and mayhem, it's about a refusal to accept illegitimate authority. Therefore I don't think an anarchist would have a major problem with the rules of the Highway Code. After all, it's no more than a convention, which on the whole provides a climate of predictability, which allows you to travel quicker than you ever could in real chaos. Figure of 8 stock car racing with no give way lines (or inclinations) at the crossroads provides spectacular sport; but it would make it difficult to give an accurate guesstimate for that SE27 to NW6, if that's what you could expect at every junction in between.

No one ends up as a traffic cop by accident; and I believe that on the whole the men and women with TD on their shoulders, do it for many of the same reasons that drew you into this business – and this has to be particularly true of those on bikes. Occasional egos and arseholes apart (which you get in every business) I think I can genuinely say that in over a quarter century of roadside interactions with bike police, very few of them have been bastards (beyond the fact that they caught me at it) while many of them have behaved like good refs, who are more than willing to play the advantage if they think you're not a total wanker.

Obviously they have to mature into it. There's nothing worse than getting a lecture from an arrogant pup who thinks he learnt more about bikes in a few months in Hendon than you've gleaned in five years hard despatching; but that's always a danger when you bestow too much authority on anyone with too few years of life experience. It requires a lot of wisdom to use power appropriately; so of course it's frustrating when you meet a youngster who's both callow and shallow, but that's just another of life's hazards; when you take your chances you accept that you may end up getting pulled by a young snot with attitude. What can I say? If you don't like the odds, stick to the traffic regulations.

Although I must say, as I get older, even the younguns seem to be getting easier to handle. My most recent encounter involved two bikes pulling me in Blackwall Lane, on the grounds that I wasn't displaying a tax disc. When I took off my lid and handed over my licence (and the tax disc from my wallet) it was obvious that I was older than the sum of both their ages. The one who was doing the talking asked if I'd ever been stopped by the police before. At which I smiled and even treated them to a good humoured chuckle, before saying that with all due respect, I'd been riding a bike for twenty-five years (I consciously avoided saying "since before either of you were born") and having spent a number of those years despatch riding, yes I had been stopped before. He said he'd thought I rode like a courier, and I asked what he was suggesting. I told him I'd seen them pull out from the petrol station right back by Greenwich baths and knew exactly where they were all the way, even when they tried to hide in my blind spot after we'd turned left. He actually apologised and said he hadn't meant that I'd committed any offences, just that I seemed to know what I was doing in traffic.

"Well that can't be all bad can it?" I pointed out with a smile which seemed to be infectious, because he agreed and nodded at his colleague to stop checking over my bike, before adding: "Have a good one", and sending me on my way.

And it's not simply a question of my age; I remember almost twenty years earlier, tearing round the North Circ and checking over my shoulder for sneaking police as I passed a downramp. Sure enough there he was, accelerating his boxer hard, preparing to swoop on me. I grabbed the front brake (not connected to the brake light on the GS425) and hauled about 40mph off my speed, which put me back under the limit. Then I waited for the tug. The cop wasn't in my mirrors, so I knew he was in my blind spot and there was no way I was going to give him the satisfaction of looking round. We continued like that for around thirty seconds before he pulled alongside and tooted. When I looked across for the inevitable finger pointing to the curb, I found instead an upraised thumb and a grin that seemed to say: "We're both playing the same game from different sides and at least you're paying attention", before he wound it on to turn off at the next junction. Clearly age is useful, but not riding like a total wanker seems to help too – I find it helps to establish common ground with the average police rider.

Occasionally you find yourself in a situation where the divisions created by generalisations break down and you realise the rider on the white bike is just another motorcyclist. Whether it's a fraternal wave out in the sticks, or a friendly chat at the traffic lights, sometimes it's obvious that they're just bikers. I remember picking my bike up, too shaken to smack the coach driver who was screaming "What sort of fucking speed were you doing there?" at me, when a police bike pulled up alongside me and the rider said, "What happened? Did the cunt pull right out in front of you?" When the driver attempted to present his angle, he was told to move it somewhere more sensible until he had time for him, or he'd be nicked for obstruction as well; then the cop turned back to me to enquire solicitously after any physical injuries "that bastard caused". Oh the brotherhood of bikers!

So next time you are pulled for something that a Gatso wouldn't even debate, don't 'dis' the ref's parents. Try instead to look past your assumptions and you might just recognise another professional rider. You never know, that moment of recognition may allow him or her to forget their own prejudices and realise they're dealing with exactly the same thing.

Be careful out there
(and remember to always keep at least two
players between you and the Gatso)
Carin' Sharin'

The Tao of Despatch
TRD issue 42 – February 2001

February 2001 saw the first incidents of foot and mouth in the UK for twenty years. Within two days of the outbreak, the EU had banned all exports of British meat, milk and livestock. Aside from the devastating cost to the farming industry caused by the slaughter of nearly four million animals, tourism was also badly hit as large sections of the British countryside were 'closed' for months.

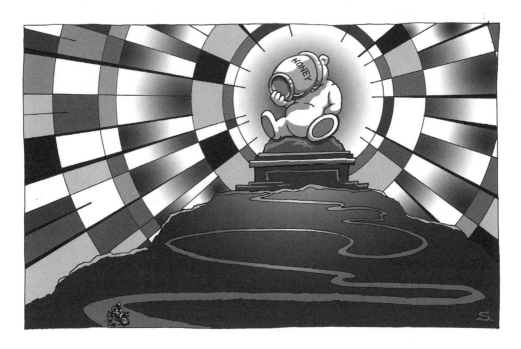

The Tao of Despatch

This month before I started off on another of my hippy meanders, I thought I'd give Roger a call to check if there was anything in particular he'd like me to ramble about. As it happened, he'd just had a conversation with the owner of a small West End company and suggested I follow it up. Apparently they'd had to get rid of a rider, because he was such a merchant of gloom he was dragging the whole firm down. In an industry where "Ability to whinge and moan" would appear to rate alongside "Comprehensive knowledge of London" as an essential prerequisite for the job, I couldn't help thinking he must have been a seriously rainy Monday.

I phoned Roger's contact and he agreed to get back to me when he had more time – but he never did. Perhaps it was all too depressing and he didn't want to have to think about it again. Phoning around various friends and associates, I got the impression that a significant slice of the industry seems to be whistling quietly to itself, while desperately trying to avoid thinking what the first symptoms of clinical depression might be. Why, I wondered, weren't there more despatch riders displaying the trademark fly-spattered teeth of the happy biker? Traffic may be heavier and certainly techno speed enforcement is becoming more intrusive month on month, but for a motorcyclist wanting to avoid the regular 9 to 5, riding a bike in one of the world's major capitals still has to be the card on the Job Centre board with the bright neon lights round it.

But if that's the case why have recruitment and retention become such problems? Could it be that for far too long recruitment was so easy that retention was never really an issue? And what's happened to slow down the steady stream of fresh young riders who can't believe their luck? There used to be shedloads of them and some of them were good for anything up to five years before the lustre began to wear thin. Maybe now that there are other jobs out there (albeit soul-destroying shit ones) they give up before they get through the often over-long introductory period, where they're expected to do shit singletons to shit postcodes, while the established riders trawl from Hammersmith to Hoxton with bulging panniers? Then again, it could be a simple like the crippling insurance premiums younger riders have to gamble with.

One thing is certain, the closer you look, the more rational reasons you can identify to account for the problem. But what if you stretch the point and look outside the sensible options? Couldn't it be the age of the business itself? Let's face it, it's very much an in-the-moment kind of trade and there's nothing like thirty years of living for the day to bring on a nasty case of mid-life crisis (with associated angst about the pointlessness of it all). So I got to thinking that perhaps what's needed is a little spirituality. Now, before Mr Ainsworth reaches for his quill, I should point out that having been raised on a staple diet of the kind of Christianity he liberally sprinkled with vitriol last month, I knew exactly where he was coming from (although I was a teenager before I became disenchanted with the sort of hypocrisy he highlighted; so his comments made me wonder if he was a pagan from birth, or did he become a 'born again' pagan on the road back from Damascus?). Personally, it took me until I was twenty before I scrubbed round the metaphysical and arrived at a kind of existential nihilism. Of course it never occurred to me that that was what it was then, because, "What the fuck?" was as close as I got to articulating my feelings at that time. I hadn't heard any of those 'big' words and even if I had, I'd have had no idea what they meant. I suppose it just seemed to me that scientific explanations (or hypotheses), while they might be suspect in all sorts of ways, still worked better than the dogma I'd been force-fed as a child.

Although I came to this attitude relatively late, I quickly realised that under those circumstances, riding a bike was the only sensible thing to do. If there is no God, no Heaven and no Hell; no right and no wrong; in fact nothing but 'the big sleep' to look forward to, why wouldn't you live for the moment? And how better than as a DR? If you're determined to live every day as if it might be your last, few jobs can really claim to deliver that possibility as reliably as yours. Even bomb disposal officers aren't out there on a daily basis, dabbing their sweating brow while they wonder whether to cut the red or the blue wire; whereas you constantly have to make life or death decisions that can be every bit as crucial as knowing which wire to clip. When a car just pulls straight out on you, you decide instantly whether to accelerate and squeeze in front of it, or brake and go for the gap that should appear if he doesn't suddenly stop when he sees you. It's the constant threats that keep you sharp and (as long as you get it right) they just feed the buzz.

Juicer, while explaining once again why a DR union ain't never gonna happen, described the massive attraction of living in the here and now; and how it allows you to ignore everything from George W. Bush to the nagging nightmare of your constantly mounting tax liability. Live fast, die young and leave a beautiful corpse (and preferably another 32 payments on your bike). Yeah, rock 'n' roll! The trouble is of course that, in spite of the best efforts of other road users and abusers, most of us live way beyond our 'best before' date.

"Live every day as if it's your last" is a good solid maxim, but it can result in some really nasty reality checks if you have too many last days and you're still around when it all goes pear-shaped. Like so many pearls of Western wisdom, it hits a spot, but it really doesn't say enough. By contrast the philosophic ruminations of Eastern sages tend to offer a broader, more holistic view; a Chinese version would surely add: "...But bear in mind that you may live for a helluva long time." It's only a small 'but', but a morsel for thought nonetheless.

There's nothing like a little Zen parable (or bastardisation thereof) to illuminate some small aspect of the meaning of life. David Morgan's contribution in last month's letters pages was a perfect example. While, as is often the case, it was tossed away in a light-hearted manner, at its heart lay a profound truth. I love things like that, because most of what I know about Eastern thinking has come from the kind of sources that any serious scholar would dismiss as trashy. Which may well be true; nonetheless calendars from

Chinese take-aways, the 70s TV series *"Kung Fu"*, and even my little 'un's book of world religions, have all given me serious pause for thought at one time or another.

You may be wondering what all this has to do with my theory that the industry is slipping into mid-life crisis (and you'd have every right to), but stick with me, I'm getting there. Once you reach an age where the days you were enjoying one at a time begin repeating themselves – in particular the shitty ones – and any attempt to pass yourself off as a young beautiful corpse would be enough to make a mourner giggle; that tends to be the time when a lot of folk start searching for something more.

As I said above, I'd had my share of 'guilt trip religion' in my youth, so becoming 'born again' wasn't really on my list. I don't mean any disrespect to anybody's religion if they're serious about it – anyone who truly lives their life with a "do unto others as you would have done unto you" attitude has my utmost respect – but, like I say, I'm with A.A. when it comes to Christmas Christians. It's interesting to consider something Bob Pirsig said in *Zen & The Art of Motorcycle Maintenance*: "...doctrinal differences among Hinduism and Buddhism and Taoism are not anywhere near as important as doctrinal differences among Christianity and Islam and Judaism. Holy wars are not fought over them because verbalised statements about reality are never presumed to be reality itself." OK the last bit explains why lots of people give up on his book, but he's got a point.

When Stevie Wonder sang, *"Heaven Is Ten Zillion Light Years Away"* in 1974, I wasn't feeling particularly spiritual, but I knew where he was coming from. Later, when I read little bits about Buddhism and Hinduism there was that sort of idea again; of God or spirituality being something inside of you, rather than something you plug into at your local religious franchise. The trouble with all that was, besides being a raw steak-eating leather-wearer, when I considered the sort of shit I'd put in it, I wasn't sure I was entirely comfortable with the idea of my body being a temple. I couldn't help imagining a dilapidated ruin with dirty clothes scattered all over and plates and mugs growing penicillin in the corners. Lots of stuff to think about though. I heard a cassette by a very clever Trevor named Krishna Murti. He propounded that Man is the only living thing that considers the concept of time passing; and we know that all the time it's passing we're dying. But when we are totally absorbed in something, time fades from our consciousness, taking with it any preoccupations we may have about our mortality. Which sounded like the perfect rationale (if I needed one) for the sort of motorcycle riding I enjoy most.

The trouble with B & H (no, not the fags) was that they were a little too religious and demanded to be taken seriously. When I realised that reaching Nirvana took more than simply humming to yourself while you smoked a joint, I knew I wasn't about to renounce all my material goods (including my bike!) so I filed away some of the more illuminating ideas they'd provided me with and carried on. Then I came across "*The Tao of Pooh*", which uses Winnie the Pooh (plus Eeyore, Christopher Robin and the rest of the crew) to introduce the reader to the principles of Taoism. If it sounds bizarre to present a fluffy yellow teddy as an analogy for a philosophy, which is almost two-and-a-half thousand years old, so be it, but it worked for me. OK, it's not the most 'cred' of books to whip out while you're standing-by in Great Marlborough Street but just like Winnie himself, it's chock-full of simple wisdom.

What appealed most about the snapshot of Taoism it gave me was that it didn't actually require me to do anything. I didn't have to subscribe to anything or give anything up; I didn't even have to start chanting or praying 16 times a day. It was simply a series of truths that were so self-evident once set out, that arguing against them would be as fruitful as trying to beat up an expert in Tai Chi. Of course that may just be my impression and I may have arrived at it because it was what I wanted, but if it hit a spot for me how bad can that be?

Essentially Taoism teaches that wisdom requires an acceptance of life's inevitable changes, while accepting that eliminating one's desires and aggressive impulses and following "The Way" will lead to a long and tranquil life. But it's not a question of following a prescribed route, it's more a case of 'going with the flow' in a more considered way. For me, Sinead O'Connor's plea: "God grant me the serenity to accept the things I cannot change, the courage to change the things I can, and the wisdom to know the difference" would find its answer in the *Tao Te Ching*.

Traffic lights are a perfect example of something you can't change. The usual traffic cycle (from green to green in your direction) is between 24 and 120 seconds, with the average around one-and-a-half minutes. It doesn't matter how much you rev, or if you clench your teeth till your brain aches, they won't change any sooner. The same goes for slow days. As long as your controller is giving you a fair shout, there's no point in giving him or her grief, it simply doesn't help. Whereas if the controller is taking the piss, that's something you can change. But, and you know this is true, the more considered you are and the calmer you are when you deal with the situation, the more satisfactory the outcome is likely to be (unless of course you've already decided that a good kicking is the only option, but that's hardly going to increase your earning potential).

I've thought for a long time that if I were to give in to my good intentions and take up some form of exercise, Tai Chi would be a lot more 'me' than jogging or aerobics. It's the one that looks like a slow-motion karate workout and I'd seen people from nine to ninety-nine doing it alone or in groups in various public places. What I had never realised, however, was that Tai Chi was also a form of self-defence. My basic understanding of it is that while exercising you are practising all the moves in perfect detail, so that if somebody attacks you, you simply speed everything up and your aggressor is left trying to work out why he keeps bouncing off you as if you've got a force field round you. I'm sorry, but from where I'm at in the fullness of my years, that strikes me as the epitome of cool.

So if I ever get around to doing anything that requires an ongoing commitment Tai Chi will be it – but another time maybe. That's the great thing about my interpretation of Winnie the Pooh's explanation of Taoism. He didn't tell me what to do with my life, nor to feel guilty about the things I know I shouldn't be doing, or the things I should doing but haven't got around to yet. All he said to me was 'If there's stuff in your life that's bothering you, take an honest look at it, and if challenging it is less trouble than continuing as things are, why not sort it?' And if it's a big thing and you can't be bothered, that's cool as well; roll another one and take it easy. Just 'go with the flow' and follow The Way as best you can.

So where exactly in all that garbled nonsense is my advice for the Despatch industry? What exactly are those of you who are wondering if Prozac will really make you better than well supposed to glean from all this waffle? Truth is I'm not sure, which is why it's all over the place. That's the trouble with the East – they're all so fucking inscrutable that nobody gives you a wink to say you've got it right. It's not about having all the answers, it's about understanding the questions.

However, if all that's a bit too enigmatic, the short version is quite simple really: lighten up. Controllers, how much empathy do you convey to your Leyton-based rider when his 6.30pm pick up going to Walthamstow turns out to be a Wimbledon? Riders, when was the last time you hugged your controller? And what about you, owners, when did you last take the whole fleet out to thank them for keeping you in the manner to which you've become accustomed? Hello? And you're wondering why things are getting a little tetchy?

You're all travelling around all day, why not make a unilateral decision to spread a little happiness as you go? Or then again don't... the choice, as always, is yours.

Be careful out there
Carin' Sharin'

The Spring of my Discontent
TRD issue 43 – March 2001

The most interesting story in March 2001 was the news of the recovery of Donald Campbell's boat Bluebird from the bottom of Coniston Water in Cumbria. It had been laying there ever since January 1967 when Campbell – the only person ever to have held both the land and water speed records at the same time – had been attempting to break his own 276mph water speed record when the vessel went out of control somersaulting repeatedly before crashing and sinking.

The Spring of my Discontent

OK, this month it's Country & Western philosophy: "Life is like a pubic hair on the side of a toilet bowl… Sooner or later you get pissed off."

Well for the first 26 years of my life I happily hung on to the clack on the side (metaphorically speaking); but by 1981 – the Spring of my Discontent – I was well and truly sluiced off. I realise for a number of you that was before you were born; but, and I realise this may come as a shock to a few of you, sex 'n' drugs 'n' rock 'n' roll aren't new things either. The songs may have changed, but the way I see it, picking up in E.15 at the arse end of a wet Friday in November, and riding to Aylesbury on a GS425 that is as soaked through and knackered out as you are, wasn't a hoot then and it's a very special sort of person who considers it their idea of fun now.

In the greater scheme of things the date's irrelevant, but those of us who were unfortunate enough to have been there will remember that the year kicked off rather ominously with John Lennon at number one, posthumously, with *Imagine*. It wasn't a bad song actually. When it was first released it had possessed an optimistic, trippy kind of resonance; but in January 1981, just a couple of months

after his untimely death, it had become an ironic epitaph. What was the line? "…
And the world could live as one." Yeah right, John.

The rest of the stuff that spewed from my radio hardly raised my spirits either.
Imagine was depressing due to circumstance rather than musical content,
whereas the shit that followed was dire. *Jealous Guy*, Roxy Music's tribute to
Lennon was the comparatively good bit, lurking as it did between Joe Dolce's
classic ditty, *Shaddup You Face*, and Shakin' Stevens' break into the BIG time, *This
Ole House* (although in reality, Brian Ferry was kinda like the crappy plastic
cheese that came between slices of stale, duffel bag-flavoured Wonderloaf in
school sarnies: interesting – but only by default). And if that lot weren't
depressing enough, Bucks Fizz, the archetypical bubbly Euro Muppets, were
lurking in the wings, twitching impatiently while they waited for Ol' Shakey to
bugger off so *Making Your Mind Up* could replace his dodgy drum as the most
played dross polluting the nation's airwaves.

It's not like radio music was the only crap in my life. Doom and gloom were
seeping in on all fronts. The political situation certainly didn't help. For two
whole years Thatcher had been strutting her stuff, flexing the collective party
muscle, and building the foundations of the society we enjoy today. At the time
I'd considered her, along with the aforementioned chart heroes, a passing
aberration – more a fly in the ointment than a serious thorn in the collective side.
If I'd suspected then how long Shakey and Bucks Fizz would have hung around,
or that the Tories would have been sleazing away for another sixteen years, I'd
probably have topped myself there and then.

Against this background of general dross, I had to go to work and suffer
controllers, pig-ignorant punters, police, jobsworths, unexpected returns,
ignored tax returns, diesel slicks, horseshit slicks, and all the other shit that
becomes such a drag when your dream job becomes a chore. For Chrissake look
how the rich and famous pop to the Priory to deal with the stress of their "jobs"
– what chance dispatching? If you started in the business because you love bikes,
what do you do when it all turns sour? By March '81 my life seemed to be
freefalling down the porcelain.

6.45pm in the Deep South (we're talking Trotter rather than Tennessee
Williams territory) and once again I lurched wearily onto the Peckham estate I
rather euphemistically called home. I locked my bike, cursed it under my breath
and hauled my various bits and pieces, along with my lethargic arse, up six

flights of foul-smelling stairs; too knackered to even check the graffiti for news.

I fumbled into the flat, and dumped my junk in the hallway before having a rather optimistic shufti in the fridge. I didn't need to replace the blown light bulb in the kitchen to see it was Mother Hubbard time, so I shuffled into the living room, switched on the TV, pitched my jacket and lid into the corner and slumped onto the sofa.

After about ten minutes I'd regained just enough strength to wrestle my waterproofs to my shins, before collapsing back into the lumpy cushions. To remove my over-trousers altogether I'd have to take my wellies off and just thinking about that made my head throb. I'd get around to that later (probably when I came to with rigor mortis at around 3.30am if recent experience was any indicator). I rolled myself a fat one and sagged still further into the couch as I lit it; then moaned wearily until even that was too much effort, so I slipped into a silent, to all intents and purposes autistic, state, where my eyes stared blankly at a point just a few inches beyond the snowy picture on the TV. The scene was getting repetitive.

When I'd started out dispatch riding back in November '78, I'd just turned twenty-four and I loved bikes. I couldn't believe anyone would give me a bike then pay me to thrash it all day. I had a company bike, money in my pocket, and within a few months I was sharing a flat with two other couriers (plus some of the most interesting degenerates in London, on a good night – and there were loads of top nights). But that was two and a half years, and more significantly, three winters earlier. Lying comatose on a lumpy couch with the box droning inanely in the corner, those days seemed as far away as the everlasting beach holidays I'd enjoyed as a seven-year-old. Things had definitely deteriorated somewhat and I was considerably less than full of the joys of spring.

Which was sad really; especially considering that elsewhere life rolled on pretty much as it always had. The spectre of winter had faded away and everywhere spring was springing. As they've done for generations, young men's testosterone-laden fancies turned once again to mating and motorcycles (and not necessarily in that order). In cities, towns, villages and hamlets across the nation, from streets, alleys, garages, kitchens and bedrooms, the pungent aromas of WD40, petrol and Castrol R were exuding slowly into the atmosphere; while the ring of tools on metal, punctuated by the occasional dull scrape of knuckles on the same, could be heard all over, combined with raucous laughter, curses (of both pain and frustration) and outrageous (if rarely more than partially true) riding stories. Bikers around the country, if not the entire Northern hemisphere, were gearing up for the good bit. The fun bit. The sunny bit!

But in a rapidly darkening room in SE15 there was no such optimism. I was fed up, pissed off, and thoroughly depressed. Sure spring had sprung, but it had come way waaay too late for me. Long before the bitter January weather had locked in, biking had ceased to be a source of pleasure. Since early autumn, every evening and from Friday night till Monday morning, my bike had stayed where it stopped. If I needed to go somewhere I'd scrounge a lift in a car, catch a bus, a train or a mini-cab – I'd even walk – anything rather than get back on the bike in my own time. The horrible truth was, I loathed riding it.

Lying there wallowing in my woes, my attention was slowly but inexorably drawn to the picture on the TV. *Top Of The Pops* had come on and there behind the snowstorm were Bucks Fizz, bouncing around and flashing their teeth like demented rabbits on wizz. I scrambled all round me purposefully, but couldn't find anything worth chucking at the TV (which was probably a good thing, as we were way behind on the rental so there was no way we'd have got yet another set out of D.E.R.). In desperation I rolled off the sofa and began crawling towards the door.

I felt as if I was towing a caravan with flat tyres. I wondered if perhaps my problems might have been entirely physiological – like anaemia or something. I dug in, redoubled my effort, and was rewarded with a searing pain in the thigh as the sofa leg gave up its grip on the buckle of my braces and – rather abruptly – allowed them to join me in my pathetic attempt to escape from the TV. I almost broke down and wept, but what was the point? Why bother? What was one more vicious torment in a life turned sour?

Frazzled, I dragged myself to the bog and climbed on; as I did it struck me that I could give up the courier game and earn a living marketing Bucks Fizz as a laxative to all the haemorrhoidal DRs. I even managed a little grimace on the strength of the idea. Bolstered by the moment of levity, I allowed myself another grin as I checked out the photos blu-tacked to the walls. In one there's a group of adrenalin-glazed bikers on a fag break in the foreground, while over their shoulders you can just make out miles of twisting mountain road. In another Woffy fills the frame wearing nothing but a chunky beer glass over his tackle and a dopey "I'm out of my skull" smile. There were various wheelies and girls on bikes, but mostly they were snaps from Le Mans, the Bol d'Or, Porthcawl,

Canvey Island, and a variety of other exotic locations; and in every one of them the people were beaming. "Happier days!" I sighed wistfully.

The curling pictures dropped out of focus, as my suffocating purple mantle slowly cascaded back down, swathing me in doom, gloom, and despondency. Yeah, happy days indeed. Well the song was wrong, they weren't here to stay. They fucked off long ago and left me hiding in a crapper. I was sitting in a five foot by four foot purgatory, getting a ring around my arse, while I wondered absently if the bog chain would take my weight. I decided it probably could, but I also figured that by the time it had lowered to the flushing position, I'd just be a poor sad bastard, standing on the floor in a chain mail necktie. Aaaaaaaaaaargh! There was no escape. I sat there with my palms squashing my eyes shut and my elbows making red marks on my thighs. TOTP was an annoying buzz in the background taunting and teasing me; a constant reminder just in case I'd missed the point, that life was in fact shit.

My low-spirited lassitude was rudely disturbed by a thunderous roar that seemed to reverberate right through me. I shuddered to think what sort of beast would make such an apocalyptic sound and I was still wrestling with that grizzly little puzzle when a sharp rap on the front door brought fresh trepidation. Curling into a foetal ball I considered trying to escape down the bog, but I decided I wouldn't be able to get round the bend (which, given my prevailing state of mind, struck me as pretty ironic), although I reckoned that at a pinch, I could probably climb in and pull the lid down.

The second, louder series of impacts rattled the window just eighteen inches behind my head. I probably only jumped a couple of feet; it seemed more, because I'm pretty sure I didn't bang my head on the ceiling. I hissed at my heart and lungs desperately, begging them to shut up and not give me away, but they were having none of it. In fact sensing my rising hysteria they lost it altogether and began running around my chest and crashing into each other in their panic.

"Come on Dave, open the door!" My paralysing paranoia disappeared as I recognised a familiar voice, only to be replaced by an equally debilitating embarrassment.

"Open up Gurwig! What are you doing, hiding in the bog!?" He thumped the window again.

"Dillon?" I played for time while I attempted to regain my composure, wipe my arse, and get dressed.

"No, the Chipping Sodbury chapter of the Hells Angels! Who the fuck do you think it is? Are you going to let me in or what?"

I opened the door rubbing my head. I'd just cracked it on the toilet wall when my waterproofs took advantage of my confusion and tripped me sneakily from behind.

"About time… What were you doing, flushing your stash down the bog?" He brushed past me and strolled into the living room.

"Why are you sitting in the dark? And what's this crap?" He snapped on the lamp, switched off Top of the Pops, and put a Squeeze tape on, before turning to survey me with a mixture of amusement and disgust as I sprawled pathetically on the couch.

"Oh for Chrissakes, you're not stumbling around with your Helly's round your ankles again Gurwig? After all the times you've been tripped over or whacked with the elastic! You're losing it. Really you're cracking up, you need to get a grip."

(As I listened to Chris Difford barking out *Cool For Cats* a note of real desperation crept into my thinking: perhaps he was right! Why hadn't it occurred to me to turn the telly off and put a tape on?)

"ARE YOU DEAF?" Dillon rapped me on the head like a teacher trying to get the attention of a lovesick teenager.

"Me?"

He took an exasperated breath before repeating slowly: 'DO… YOU… WANT… TO… SEE… MY… LATEST?'"

"Oh er yeah, right. Roger Rog… Erm, lead on MacDuff!" He gave me a very weird sideways glance before striding out to the front door, leaving me desperately trying to get it together as I waddled along in his wake. For almost an hour before his arrival I'd been wrapping myself in a six-skin blanket of neurosis and paranoia; consequently with his sudden matter-of-fact arrival, I was having considerable trouble finding an outcrop of reality to bung an anchor on.

He stood on the balcony looking into the courtyard. Turning back towards me he waved me along good-naturedly, as I shuffled pathetically down the hall. His expression showed pity and humour in equal parts and he put his arm around my shoulder to guide my last few faltering steps. Sweeping his arm in a grand gesture he indicated the courtyard three floors below: "Behold!"

I ground my eyes with my knuckles, before opening them squinting. There among the rusting heaps on bricks, the primer-ed Datsuns and Toyotas, and the tarted-up Escorts, was an unadulterated vision of loveliness in silver and blue. She was magnificent. Long, lithe, and unbelievably sensual. Even in the fading light and the pathetic glimmer of the few lamps that weren't smashed, there was no mistaking her incredible beauty, elegance, and class.

"You coming down?" He said smiling beatifically.

"Yeah, just let me get these off!"

You'd have thought Debbie Harry had walked onto the landing and told me to drop my kit the way I plonked to the chilly floor and tore off my Helly's and wellies. I rushed off in my socks and was as blissfully unaware of the coldness of the floor as I was of the piss stains in the stairwell. As I rounded the second then the first landings, I quickly checked that the apparition hadn't spirited herself away and as I strode across to the spot where Dillon stood glowing proudly, even the crunching gravel and dog shit failed to register.

My face had the slightly vacant, but peaceful and contented expression you tend to find on born again Christians. I had been to the very edge of the abyss of existential angst and had a good long shufti down the hole. But now I was saved. I realised that there was the possibility of motorcycling life after dispatch riding!

I sat on Dillon's Ducati 900SS and an overwhelming feeling of serenity eased through me. As I placed my shoeless feet onto the cold knurled metal of the rearsets and stretched across to caress the clip-ons, the bar-end mirror filled with crimson and indigo as the sun slipped demurely behind the North Peckham Estate. I sucked in the balmy spring air and, rather than cause Ray any further distress, sang in my head:

"Happy days are here again,
Da de-da de da da da
Da de-da de da da da
Happy days are here agaaiin!!"

Be careful out there
Carin' Sharin'

... Made Glorious Summer by this Duke of Yorkshire

TRD issue 44 – April 2001

Talk about hell hath no fury like a woman scorned, in a story that was completely unrelated to the title of my article, Jane Andrews – a former personal assistant to the Duchess of York – went on trial accused of murdering her millionaire boyfriend by bashing him on the head with a cricket bat then stabbing him with a kitchen knife – and all because he refused to marry her!

... Made Glorious Summer
by this Duke of Yorkshire

Last month, after spending three pages describing a grey world where purple was the only hint of a tint, it all ended with a glorious burst of Technicolor. You'd be forgiven for questioning how credible it was that a motorcycle, even a classically beautiful example like the Ducati 900SS, could have such a profound effect on someone's mental state. Well of course it can't; certainly not if you're clinically depressed. Consequently I admit that I deserve a few points on my poetic licence for last month's effort (and if I knew where to send the dosh I'd pay the fines).

I don't claim any expertise when it comes to depression; but if I understand anything I'm clear that the most debilitating thing is the total inability to see any escape from your predicament. As my problems at the time centred largely on despatching, which had ground away my love of biking, the issues were nothing that a change of job wouldn't have sorted. But I did feel stuck, because I'd got used to earnings I couldn't hope to match elsewhere. Once my love affair with bikes had soured (as any relationship will when too much shit happens over too long a period and there seems little danger of anything fresh or new happening) I did feel well and truly trapped.

Dillon's Duke literally blew away my blues. The realisation that here was a friend who worked at the same company as me, who earned no more than I did, but who was able to ride such a rare and wonderful thing, was like a light bulb in a cartoon character's head. I'd known instantly that it was exactly what I needed. Simply sitting on it had reignited my spark and the voice shouting, "Do it! Do it! Do it!" in my head was joined by all the supposedly sensible parts agreeing that if Ray could afford the finance on a brand new one, surely I could borrow enough wonga for a second-hand one in black and gold.

So it was that, less than a week later, I found myself boarding a train at King's Cross with my lid in my hand and two grand in my pocket. I was heading so far north of Watford that I knew from the problems I'd had with the guy on the phone that I was likely to struggle to communicate with the locals, so I stepped off the train in Bradford and got straight into a cab, handing the driver the address on a slip of paper. He delivered me to a development of prim semis with attached garages. After paying him, I turned to find a Kevin and Sharon sort of couple standing in the doorway.

They told me how they only used it on sunny Sundays and how they'd toured to the South of France on it. They were still rabbiting in their curious dialect with its soft 'U's and hard 'A's, when the garage door swished up and turned them into background noise – like the hiss on a cheap tape. There in the spacious interior stood the object of my dreams and in the flesh (or aluminium, fibreglass and steel to be more precise) it was so much better than I had ever imagined.

I walked around the Duke in a semi trance. It was all there: the black and gold paintwork; the big in-line 90° cylinders (with the Desmo's bevel drives running up the offside); the 40mm Dellortos complete with caged bellmouths; and the straight-through Contis. The Avon Roadrunners and luggage rack were a bit jarring and they brought Tracy and Darren's voices back into focus in time for me to figure that he was asking if I wanted to wheel it oot and start it oop. I was about to say "Does the Pope shit in the woods?", but thought it would only cause confusion, so I settled for, "Yeah, great".

Once it was running and I was sitting on it gently tweaking the quick-action throttle and listening to the twin-cylinder symphony rise and fall, I was sold, and so was the Duke. £1,950; thank you very much and goodbye.

Winding my way from Stacy and Warren's place in the 'burbs it all felt a bit strange. The powertrain seemed to snatch, the lack of steering lock was terrifying, and the suspension (which I'd been warned had inspired *Stiff Records'* motto: "If it ain't Stiff it ain't worth a fuck") felt like Viagra-plus – and all my weight was sitting on my wrists. However, as I left the residential streets behind and rolled it open on a short stretch of dual carriageway it all began to make sense; and by the time I'd rounded and exited my first roundabout I was feeling a tingling in my loins.

I quickly found my way through Bradford and Leeds and onto the M1. Back then there was no way I'd risk trying to find some interesting A and B roads home – not that far into the great unknown – there'd be plenty of time for that once I was back on familiar ground in the South East. Which is where I wanted to be, because London was where my friends were, and they were waiting to see it. So I checked my watch, pointed it down the big One, gave it a squirt and felt the surge of power. 110mph was totally effortless and the weight evaporated from my wrists, leaving me free to revel in the moment as I wafted south.

After about half an hour of roaring past all and sundry at one-ten, I hit a clear-ish stretch and tucked in behind the fairing to see what it had. The 130mph it was geared for wasn't spectacular even by 1981 standards – there were a number of Jap bikes with claimed higher top speeds, but they all needed a long straight bit of road to reach it. Snapping the throttle open on the Dellortos activated Super-Squirter-sized accelerator pumps that caused it to lunge forward as if it was doing eighty. It hit one-thirty in a rush and was urging me to explore the red, but the realisation that I'd just paid more for my wonderful Italian stallion than I'd ever paid for anything in my life persuaded me to fight the temptation and keep it shy of the danger line. I noticed a 'Services 1 mile' sign and less than half a minute later I was admiring the feel of the Brembos as I pulled off the motorway. It was all getting a bit too much and I was afraid I was going to explode at the gut-busting excitement of it all. I knew I needed to sit down, calm down, and stop getting so carried away. There was no point in buying a Ducati, then mortally wounding my licence before I'd even taken it near the sort of roads it was designed for.

I'd brought no locks, so I sat where I could keep a close eye on my new toy while I ate. Besides, I wanted to be able to admire it. Who wouldn't? But as I watched I was genuinely amazed to see just how many people of all ages stopped to look it over as they walked in or out; and it was clear that many of those arriving were partially interested to see what it was that had blurred past them back up the road some. I'd bought the 900SS because of all the reports I'd read describing its prodigious handling and stomping power delivery. Obviously the fact that I'd always considered it to be the most beautiful machine ever built played its part, but until that moment I honestly hadn't given any serious thought to pose value. That said, I'd be a liar to claim that I didn't get a massive bang out of it once it became apparent.

Walking back to the Duke with food, drink, nicotine, urine, and adrenaline all back at ambient levels, I was ready to rock 'n' roll. However, as I prepared to kick it over, it occurred to me that although I'd paid close attention when I was shown, I'd never actually attempted to start it myself. At the same moment I became aware that I had quite an audience watching from behind the glass of the eatery. I set it up, squirted the pumps, kicked sharply and was rewarded with a roar that left my cool bike-god act intact; so I burbled over to the filling station to fuel up.

Four early shifts saw me back on the main carriageway. The rumble grew steadily as I crossed the first two lanes, before settling at a fierce growl by the time I hit the outside lane doing a ton-ten. I'd love to enthral you with every minute detail of that ride, but the truth is I can't remember a single thing about it. However, this has absolutely nothing to do with the twenty years that have raced past on nitro since that day. When I pulled up in SE14 (barely two and a half hours' riding time after joining the M1 in Leeds) and attempted to respond to a barrage of questions, my mind was blank. My mates, who'd heard me coming down the Old Kent Road and rushed out of the Crown & Anchor to meet me, had crowded round demanding to hear every detail. Which was when I realised I had absolutely no recollection of anything – just an overwhelming feeling of awe and exhilaration.

It was like being woken from a dream and being asked to describe it. You know that moment when you wake and the fantastic REM world you've been embroiled in is still there in every part of your body and mind; but when you attempt to interpret it, it pops like a bubble leaving you with nothing but the residue of feelings – fear, ecstasy, lust, whatever – associated with the almost memory. I think the same must apply to riding bikes.

When you're practising RMM (Rapid Motorcycle Movement) on busy thoroughfares, whether it's the M1 or Knightsbridge, you have to be entirely focussed. To travel seriously faster than the surrounding traffic, the whole of your brainpower needs to be allocated to processing the mass of information that your senses require to avoid disaster. 130mph on an M road is (pedestrians aside) the equivalent of racing through Asda's car park at sixty. You have to be absolutely tuned in to everything: your immediate surroundings (including the periphery and your mirrors); the middle distance; and a horizon that constantly rushes to meet you. I believe that your inboard computer shuts down all hard disc functions and forgets all about keeping a record, because it knows it needs to convert everything available to RAM, so it can deal with all the random shit coming your way. Which would also account for why, when I arrived in New Cross, aside from my lack of memories, I was also aware that since leaving the services I hadn't had a single thought that wasn't directly associated with riding. Not about my dinner, my waiting friends, what I was doing that evening, not even what the red-head receptionist in Neal Street would look like naked – nothing but the task in hand.

And how was that task? As far as chores go, it was a bit like being Julianne Moore's love slave! Beyond that, given my meagre abilities with the written word, I'd struggle to begin to do justice to the joy that my new-found love provided me with. Suffice it to say that while last month's tale of depression may have been something of an exaggeration, I was definitely down, but the moment I got rolling on the Duke it dragged me out of it at two miles a minute. There was none of the slow process of therapy, or of waiting for tricyclic drugs to kick in; it was an instant spike in the vein.

I went back to work and although I was on the GS425 everything was different. It was as if I'd been rinsed through and all the negative shit that had been silting up for months had been flushed out, leaving me appreciating once again what an amazing job I had. I couldn't imagine what the problem had been. Looking through fresh eyes I'd reacquainted myself with just how effective the GS was around town. I was determined not to use the Duke for despatching. Not because of any practical considerations; I simply wasn't about to risk ruining my budding beautiful relationship by exposing it to the sort of over-familiarity and abuse it would inevitably suffer on the DR circuit. Besides, it would have felt like taking a lover who'd introduced me to previously unimagined heights of passion and pleasure and putting her on the game. I used the 900SS occasionally, but always as a treat. If a decent job came up, it was only a short bop to Peckham, which made it just like dashing home to get your best gal when you've picked up a good run to the seaside or out to the country.

What about the downside? I guess there are always people out there who want to know about faults; but for me anyone looking for negatives in the face of something so close to personal perfection simply doesn't understand the nature of true love. It's a bit like saying that Ms Moore's gorgeous, intelligent, and incredibly passionate and everything... but she sometimes has dodgy bed-breath in the morning! I say "Negatives, smegatives!" The engine, suspension and brakes always delivered superbly, so any time I felt a need for speed, or in the teeniest bit down, or at a loss, all I had to do was wrap myself around my soul-mate and head for open roads – and it *always* took me to a better place.

For me, the 900 Desmo was already God's own motorcycle – as much as any man could hope for. But then, a couple of weeks after I bought it, I pulled up in Neal Street to pick up a 9am booking to Hereford, and my favourite fantasy, red-head, came outside and, after asking if I minded, hitched up her short, tight, skirt and wriggled onto the pillion, then leant against me and asked if I'd like to give her a ride sometime...

Did my Ducati make me happy? Are bears Catholic?!

Be careful out there
Carin' Sharin'

Hollywood Ending
TRD issue 46 – June 2001

In June there was yet more royal fury centred on the subject of marriage; Crown Prince Dipendra of Nepal, after arguing with his mum over his choice of bride, stomped off to his room only to return with a couple of machine guns, with which he then proceeded to massacre eleven members of his family, including his parents the King and Queen. It was the largest number of royalty killed at one time since the Bolsheviks slaughtered the Russian royal family in 1918.

UNITED WE STAND...
UNITED WE STAND...
UNITED WE STAND...
UNITED WE STAND...
UNITED WE STAND...
UNITED WE STAND...
UNITED WE STAND, DIVIDED WE FALL.
UNITED WE STAND, DIVIDED WE FALL.
MUST GET UNITED WITH SOMEONE... PREFERABLY A REDHEAD.
S.

Hollywood Ending

In last month's "From the Editor" slot, Roger bemoaned the erosion of any sense of community in the despatch industry. However, he qualified his negativity by explaining that he'd just had yet another bike nicked, which allowed the possibility that his perspective was warped by the fact that, even on tiptoes, he might have been having trouble peering out of his pit of despair. But I've got to say, even from the standpoint of a man whose biking life is on a bit of a roll at the moment, all the evidence seems to point in precisely that direction.

Exactly a year ago in a piece entitled "Once More For The Road", I thought I put an irrefutable case for a riders' union. I finished by offering to run a Blue Peter-style meter, to provide readers with a visual monthly indication of the level of interest. The problem is any "Interestmeter" or graph needs to have at least two dimensions, but by the time I next sat down to write, all I had was a baseline with a big zero written alongside it. I thought of all sorts of smartarse ways of presenting my 1D model and giving you the readership a good bollocking for your apathy and total lack of foresight, but in the end I decided to drop it. I figured that if that's the way life is nowadays, the last thing you need is me nagging you when you're sitting down for a dump. Instead I wrote a piece about stuffing bikes while ogling redheads, beautiful breasts and a range of similar distractions – and I got stacks of feedback!

This confirmed something I'd suspected all along and at the same time let me off the hook. I'd given it my best shot and there were no takers, so I was free to get on with the more hedonistic bits of life with a clear conscience. It wasn't like I'd started out with an "I'm alright Jack, sod 'em" attitude, I'd really tried. I had to because I believe to my marrow in the principle of strength through unity. I was raised on a diet of Sunday after-roast TV films like "It's a Wonderful Life" and "The Grapes of Wrath", which reinforced the idea that if we all pulled together and worked cooperatively we could overcome any adversity – and I bought it all, hook, line and sinker. Even today the scene where thousands of slaves stand up one at a time and declare, "I'm Spartacus!" still brings a lump to my throat, because corny or clichéd as the idea may be, I know that ultimately it's true: united we stand, divided we fall.

In the Sixties and Seventies when the chant of "The workers, united, will never be defeated!" rang out, the men and women who shouted it knew it was true and so did their employers. That's why post 1979, Thatcher's number one priority was to smash the unions, because none of her government's serious long-term policies (policies that irrevocably changed the face of this country) could be enacted until that had been achieved. The 1984 Miners' Strike was the last pitched battle of the class war – and in case you missed the news, our side lost. The Tories threw literally billions at it, because they could not afford to lose (although if you read Seumas Milne's staggering *"The Enemy Within"* you'll realise just how close they came to defeat). After the miners, Wapping was no more than a skirmish. The printers were out and there were always going to be more than enough police to ensure that, with the help of TNT, Murdoch was able to punt out tits and the *Times*, with the absolute minimum of overheads for maximum profits.

It's hardly surprising that folk nowadays are less inclined to believe they have an ability to affect their own lives when so many things are simply imposed on them by outside interests. Apart from massively expensive fictional stories produced on celluloid by some of the richest multi-nationals on the globe, you rarely see examples of 'people power' winning through – not in real life; not these days. Which is hardly surprising when you consider how effectively big business, politics, and the media have stitched everything up in the last twenty years. Even on the rare occasions when there have been victories against the status quo, it's hardly any great surprise that the media Barons (i.e. some of the richest and most powerful people in the world) chose not to make a song and dance about it.

That's why Roger asked me to write this piece. Although it has absolutely nothing to do with bikes, it's a 100% true story about a community taking on the Big Bad guys – multi-nationals, politicians and property developers – and beating the arrogant sonsofbitches! The reason I was asked to write this is because I'm proud to be a part of that community and to have done my own tour of duty in a fight, which for some has lasted as long as the First World War!

I've lived in Crystal Palace along with my family for the last nine years. I'm a North London boy gone native and I love it. Aside from the area's stunning views across London (Kent, Surrey and even Essex on a clear day) its greatest asset is a real sense of community. My boys walk to their tiny primary school in five minutes, as do most of their mates. It's a local school and the kids who go there represent a perfect cross-section of the local population. Their parents' social standing ranges from single mums on council estates, to loaded but liberal professional couples in big houses across on the Dulwich side; but if you saw the boys and girls doing their kiddie thing at playtime, you'd struggle to say who belonged to whom.

I'm not claiming I live in Shangri-La on the high slopes of Upper Norwood, but considering we're bringing up kids in London in the 21st Century, I really can't grumble. So when I found out six years after moving to the area that there was a plan to build an enormous multiplex about fifty feet from my patio doors I was more than a little perturbed. Especially when I found out that I, along with the rest of the local population, had already been consulted and apparently we'd all agreed it was absolutely fine and groovy. The more I found out the more it reminded me of the beginning of the late Douglas Adams' *Hitch-Hiker's Guide To The Galaxy*, when it was announced that the Earth was about to be demolished to make way for an Intergalactic Highway.

They planned to build the 20-screen horrorplex – the biggest in the Southeast – on the site of the old Crystal Palace, alongside the TV mast at the top of the park, which would require clearing the highest tree-lined ridge in south London. I'm hardly a tree hugger and I love going to the cinema. I'm certainly no NIMBY (there's a Care In The Community home less than twenty feet from my front door for Chrissake, and a number of the residents seem to have conditions that require them to scream and wail on a semi-regular basis, but that's community, I can live with that). But when some arrogant Masonic hand-shakers in Bromley decide that me, my family, and all the other insignificant people in the area are going to get shafted, simply because developing our park is too good a business opportunity to miss, and that when it came down to it, the only choice we had was whether we took it with or without lubrication, my first reaction was to say: "Are they bollocks!" and my second was to find out where to join the resistance

The Eco-Warriors (that's crusties to you) fought them heroically in the trees and their tunnels, which kept the issue in the media spotlight and galvanised community support. The Crystal Palace Campaign (the Great and the Good of the Dulwich Set) arranged and/or financed many events; more significantly, they fought the development along every conceivable avenue of the political and legal systems, and although they were denied at every level. As long as they were slapping appeals in, no trees on the site got chopped. Then there was Diane Barker, a local single mum, who got Legal Aid and took the British Government to the European Court for failing to carry out an environmental assessment – and won!

For my part, I helped start the Boycott UCI group, and our mission was to fuck with UCI's public image by drawing attention to their involvement in the deal. We formed the group after a demonstration in March 1999, when over 1,500 members of the local community turned up at the Empire Leicester Square, before marching on Downing Street and handing in a massive petition; and members of our team have been picketing the Empire once a week ever since. We focussed on causing UCI maximum embarrassment and we'd turn up whenever the media were in attendance (i.e. at premieres) or we'd send out press releases inviting them to a variety of stunts from birthday parties outside the Empire each March, to a National Boycott UCI Day, when supporters and flying pickets descended on UCI cinemas and multiplexes right across the UK.

Whenever I was involved in a public demo, picket or whatever, there'd be loads of lovely caring folk queuing to sign our petitions, but the ones that really lifted my heart were the bad guys and cynics who'd initially stride past like you're some pathetic placard-wielding saddo, before catching a tossaway line and turning back. It always went something like: "Hang on, run that by me again. This lot are going to build a fucking great cinema with 20 screens – what's the point in that, when they don't even make 20 good films a year? – in Crystal Palace Park!? Isn't that the one with the dinosaurs and the kids' farm and all? I remember going there on a picnic with my primary school – pukka park. That's a load of bollocks, where do I sign?"

While that isn't a direct quote, it's a reasonable distillation of the sort of response I tended to get from Londoners who were initially uninterested. I found that if you could just get past their assumption that you were an anorak with nothing better to do than try to save the planet, invariably they'd listen and the issue spoke for itself. But ultimately I didn't mind what people thought I was because, in common with many of the people involved in the action, my life had been ticking along just nicely until all this shit came along. Which was why we were so determined to fight it. It wasn't a question of property prices, I wasn't planning to sell, I like where I live and I wasn't about to allow commercial interests to just waltz in and ruin it. At times it was a struggle to maintain the struggle, but I always found reassurance in the certain knowledge that the community, united and with right on its side, really would never be defeated.

I met many people who actively supported our cause, who would declare point blank that they were doing so on a matter of principle, because in reality there was absolutely no way this development could actually be stopped. The sums involved were simply too big (megamillions) so it was obvious the fix had to be well and truly in. Besides, Bromley Council had already fronted up over two mill for the Eco evictions, and Central Government were planning to plough regeneration money into it, so it wasn't going to go away. It was simply a matter of time until the dodgy coalition of undeclared vested interests won through and stomped all over the local population's interests.

While the forces of evil (government ministers, councillors, the developers and UCI) may have put it differently, that's precisely the line they'd maintained all the way through. It was going to happen, because there was simply too much riding on it. Then a fortnight ago, entirely out of the blue, Bromley released a press statement saying they were throwing in the towel. Alright that's not how they put it. They dressed it up in all sorts of bollocks and stated their biggest concern was for the local people who would now be unable to get crap minimum wage polyester uniformed jobs in the development, but the bottom line was inescapable – they'd quit. We'd run 'em and scored a major popular victory!

When Russell Crowe led his gladiators to victory in the recent Oscars, it was simply the latest, most expensive version of the old "united we stand" line that Hollywood has been cynically churning out since it first recognised that mug punters like to see that sort of stuff, because like glamour, it's something that seems to be missing in their everyday lives. I was already involved in this fight long before Ridley Scott's epic hit the screens and I didn't need a more refined, formulaic re-hash of the impossible dream. I'd already got the moral in Frank Capra and John Ford's versions as a kid. They'd convinced me such a victory was possible, I'd just never believed I would actually be a part of one

There's a line in *"The Enemy Within"* which really struck a chord when I first read it: "Many said they would do it all again and many had clearly enjoyed the experience; they had lived at a pitch, physically, intellectually, morally even, which they could not expect to again, and which most who have not undergone war would never emulate." George Orwell, who was wounded in the Spanish Civil War, made a similar observation when recalling his time on the Aragón front: "… One realised afterwards that one had been in contact with something strange and valuable. One had been in a community where hope was more normal than apathy or cynicism, where the word 'comrade' stood for comradeship and not, as in most countries, for humbug."

Although our battle for the high ground in Crystal Palace hardly bears comparison with the life or death struggles those quotes refer to, they kept flashing through my mind as I came to terms with what we – a community which should have been powerless to resist – had achieved. Our dogged fight really had drawn in people of every age and background, from designer-clothed toddlers to hard-up pensioners; and we all knew it was us who'd cracked it, not the politicians who grovel for our support once every four or five years.

By the time you see this, another General Election will have come and gone and you'll know which bunch have been most successful at sucking up to the ever-dwindling number of people who still believe the political process holds any relevance for them. Given the overall climate and Roger's moans last month, it's unlikely that many of you will have bothered to set off early, or have taken time at the end of a hard day to cast your vote on the long shot that it might have any noticeable impact on your life – and to be honest I wouldn't blame any of you who arrived at that conclusion. It's ironic that the more involved you get, the more you realise that politics is nothing but a front to ensure that business is free to get on with making profits.

You won't have seen our victory splashed all over the press and TV because, unless it's featuring at a multiplex near you, 'people power' really isn't any good for profits. However, if you've any doubts about the effectiveness of a united front, next time you're out in the open somewhere in London, take a look up at the Eiffel tower of the south and check what's alongside it. What do you see? An ugly concrete monstrosity or a couple of hundred trees? Right, now tell me what a community can't achieve when they stand together.

In case you missed the news, our side won this one!

Be careful out there
Carin' Sharin'

Ron's Story
TRD issue 47 – July 2001

The New Labour government was defeated in the Houses of Parliament for the first time since they rose to power in 1997. Although Blair had been re-elected in a landslide victory only weeks earlier, over a hundred labour MPs voted against the sacking of Donald Andersen and Gwyneth Dunwoody as chairs of select committees. Apparently the rebellious MPs had been angered by attempts to rig the membership of watchdog committees and other forms of "control freakery" by the executive.

Ron's Story

As he crested the hill and hit the downgrade Ron saw a comparatively clear stretch of motorway opening up ahead of him. He tugged on the throttle of his CB550K and felt it take on a harder edge as it accelerated to 90mph. It had been a great run; motorway, man, and machine as one. He was wired. Not jumpy, just completely tuned in to what he was doing, which was moving quickly alongside a mass of potentially lethal humanity in heavy metal boxes.

That's why his adrenaline hit boost the very first millisecond that his front tyre exploded. From that moment everything moved in ultra slow motion as his well-tuned motorcycling brain moved into full survival mode. The bike went through momentary contortions that seemed to last for minutes but were actually over in a blur, before going into an enormous high-side which threw him at the tarmac at a speed in excess of 80mph.

Ron holds an international racing licence, so he knew there was nothing to do but let it all go loose and hope that it was only friction that slowed him down. As he skipped, bumped and slid along the outside lane of the M27, his eyes stayed with the bike, as it pitched and ricocheted down the road. It did five complete flips, as it went through its slow-mo ballet of destruction; and he watched in awe as the tank crumpled flat in a single bounce. The fourth one took care of his girlfriend's lid, which disintegrated under the weight of the Honda. He winced inwardly. In another half hour it would have been strapped to her chin, instead of the seat. The surge of relief that came with the realisation that whatever happened he didn't have to worry about her allowed him to forget for a moment that the only thing that was gradually slowing him down was the grippy surface grinding away the flesh of his right hip.

A thoroughly seasoned brain in full alert mode is a wonderful thing. It'll shift through your options in nanoseconds; but on a major artery the biggest danger facing you is all the motorway zombies steaming up right behind you – and they're beyond your control. Clearly Ron's defences decided they could do nothing while he was bumping and skidding at the sort of speed that human bodies simply weren't designed for and that the best they could manage would be to focus on his rapidly mangling bike, to keep his mind off all the grizzly possibilities heading his way.

As he slowed, he wondered almost absently if any of the pain that rushed in from all points indicated injuries which would prevent him from running or diving for safety; but as he came to a halt and looked behind him all he saw was a couple of hundred yards of empty tarmac. Beyond that stood three lanes of stationary vehicles with hazard lights flashing and a tailback which stretched half way up the hill and kept on growing. Meanwhile a jam sandwich raced across the gap and ground to a stop literally seconds behind him.

While the police made him comfortable and coned off the area, they explained that they'd been nicking someone on the hard shoulder and had actually seen the puff of dust as his tyre burst. They were sprinting towards him with blues and twos going and calling for an ambulance almost before he hit the ground. And the traffic? Apparently the driver of the artic Ron had just passed, had also seen the tell tale dirt fly. He'd hit his hazard lights immediately and swayed across all three lanes of the carriageway, which had the desired effect of bringing the trailing traffic to a terrified screeching halt.

The police didn't identify the razor-sharp trucker, so Ron never got the opportunity to thank him, which he regretted, because remarkably, he was able to limp out of hospital eight hours later, with a load of wadding stuffed in his right hip, but nothing broken. He was under absolutely no illusion that the driver's quick thinking and instant decisive action was the crucial factor that had ensured that his horrific spill hadn't turned into a terminal tragedy.

Be careful out there
Carin' Sharin'

Restoration Comedy
TRD issue 48 – August 2001

While Hollywood's 'golden couple' Tom Cruise and Nichol Kidman were going their separate ways after an LA divorce (which it was being rumoured was likely to cost the diminutive Cruiser something in the region of $100m), tarnished former Conservative MP Neil Hamilton and his wife Christine, were standing firm and united against the accusation that they had been involved in a serious sexual assault.

Restoration Comedy

If you've read much of the stuff I've written in TRD, you'll know I ride a rotting old SRX6 which, aside from being my daily transport, has until very recently, been my only source of motorcycling jollies. Last October in issue 38, I described how my headlight fell off on a pitch-black back road in Wales. What I failed to mention was that it wasn't alone. So many bits had vibrated loose by the time I got back to SE19 that I realised I'd been in more danger of being pulled for littering than speeding. Nonetheless, just like John Wayne with half a dozen bullets in his chest, the 16-year-old Yamaha continued to slog on manfully. In return, I'm ashamed to say, I failed to deliver anything by way of meaningful maintenance; not even first aid. In a nutshell, I mercilessly abused its big-hearted willingness.

In spite of all the shit and my apparent indifference to its welfare, the SRX has stood by me loyally for over three and a half years. It's like some oriental Tammy Wynette, who's man keeps doing her wrong, but who just keeps on struggling – and all for the sake of the occasional good legover (the irony being that even then, it's the desperately flogged and abused bike that puts in all the lung-busting effort). Day after day without exception, whenever I called on it, it always started; and whether it rattled, coughed, or growled, it always got me to my destination.

As time went on, I realised that whenever I made that statement, I made it more out of sheer amazement than any sense of pride. I knew that there was no way it could continue to maintain its Herculean effort. As hard as I tried to duck reality until I had a bit more time, or my finances were in a less dire state, I was well aware that the day was long overdue when it would simply breathe a sigh and die. I also knew that if there was any justice in the world, it would choose a desolate B road somewhere in the middle of nowhere to do it. By March, it had got to the stage where I was scared to go to my Mum's in Kentish Town in case I didn't make it back to pick my boys up from school. The situation had got ridiculous. Unless I had nothing on for the whole day, I wouldn't go further than up the road and back; and fun runs became a thing of the past.

The trouble is I've always had a bit of a "never put off until tomorrow, what you can put off until the day after" sort of attitude; with the result that I rarely get around to fixing things until they finally break down. Whenever I had a day off and thought I really must do something, anything, even if only to show willing, I'd look at the Yam and so many areas would scream for urgent attention that there seemed little point in twiddling around the edges – so I wouldn't. Instead, I'd sit on the doorstep and have a smoke while I pondered the enormity of the task.

The whole bike was liberally smeared in oil. There were tell-tale gungey rings at the top of both fork legs; the rear shocks were black and gritty, indicating (if the "bouncy" ride hadn't already tipped me off) that their contents had oozed down the outside; and the engine, in particular the left side, looked like a chip pan from the *"Young Ones"*. The major source of engine oil was hardly a major mystery, the base gasket had been blowing since before I went to Wales; but then one day I discovered that the bolt whose job it was to nip it down at the nearside rear of the barrels had lost its head. That's not to say that it started humming S Club 7 songs; claiming that New Labour where the answer to all of our problems; or suggesting the 250 Superdream was the best machine Honda ever produced; I mean it had actually lost the six-sided bit that was meant to be torqueing down that corner of the engine. How or when it went, I've no idea. One day I was just watching the mini-bubbles that always gurgled from the base when I warmed it up and I noticed it was gone!

It was the same sad story wherever you looked. I'd become used to other bikers giving me accusatory stares at traffic lights, because it really was a mess. The logbook stated that the bike was silver, but the tank (which I'd got from a breakers in Wolverhampton after the original one rotted through) was canary yellow and had developed that arty cracked effect you get on old masters. The SuperTrapp exhaust, which was the best thing on the bike, covered the offside pillion peg, while the looped bracket that (usually) stopped it detaching itself was an incredibly ugly lash-up. Every surface on the bike was covered in grime, corrosion, or oxidisation; most with all three.

The problem was I knew I needed to put a fair chunk of time aside; and that was in almost as short supply as money (although fortunately you can't quite go overdrawn with time!). Last time I rebuilt the Yam, that's literally what I did: I put it back together. I took it apart around six months before, after a bracket broke on the exhaust; but when I tried to sort it out, I discovered so many knackered or rotten bits that I had no choice but to take the engine out. I finished up stripping the whole top end down; but then I hit a brick wall trying to get the worn head sorted. Luckily, Simon Pavey loaned me the XR600 he did the Paris/Dakkar on; so my motor ended up spending half a year waiting for me to get the bits and my act together.

Unsurprisingly, it took until Si needed to give the bike back to Honda before I finally got my shit together and tracked down everything I needed, including a new secondhand head. Then, as I say, I put it back together. For many of you that may be bread and butter, but I've got to say for me it was an unbelievable feat. I was genuinely amazed when it started and ran; and I would never have believed (and certainly wouldn't have taken any bets) that it would continue to do so for another two years. But against all odds, that's exactly what it did. It continued to pile on the kilometres; and on its second anniversary this Easter, it was still defiantly limping along.

That's when I had my day out on a CBR1000, courtesy of Project Bike. I'd just dropped it off and was plodding home back on my bike when I got into a pointless thing with a VTR. I was just up the road from my house when he wheelied away from the lights, and I ended up tearing straight past my street at a silly speed. I was chasing him all the way until he turned back up Gypsy

Hill; then all he did was tip the front wheel skyward, before gunning it up the sharp incline – and that was it. In the traffic and going downhill, I was fighting an uphill battle, but going up a steep hill, I was doing nothing at all.

I rode back to my house at a more sensible speed, relieved that none of my neighbours seemed to have noticed me being childish in my own backyard. I sat on the doorstep smoking again, and looked across at my bike as it stood there panting and bleeding. I knew this just couldn't go on. I needed to either sort my bike out, or bite the bullet and get a new one. Mindful of all the beautifully restored bikes I'd seen at Project Bike, I knew exactly what I had to do. You can only procrastinate for so long before it becomes inescapable that it's a long way past the day after the day after tomorrow, and that you're pushing your luck. The moment when a little timely maintenance would have bought me another couple of years was long past; so if I was going to do anything with my bike, I needed to do it all.

Obviously, the engine would require a full rebuild (preferably started and finished within the same calendar year). All the rotten, rounded-off bolts would need to be surgically removed so that they, along with the rest of the mild steel fittings, could be trashed and replaced with stainless Allen jobbies. The tank needed some damage repair; then, once some kind of consensus had been reached, the whole bike needed a paint job. The nearside indicators were held together by insulating tape, so the whole lot needed to go in favour of something a little neater. Then there were the brakes: all three callipers needed stripping and servicing (don't we all) and while I was at it, I knew it wouldn't do any harm to bung on anodised and braided hoses. The SuperTrapp was waay too good to imagine life without; but ideally it would be nice to have the option of sharing the pleasure with a pillion occasionally. After that lot the suspension seemed like a simple prospect.

I know there are those of you who enjoy the details: all the hours spent rubbing down paint, grinding valves and drilling out broken studs; the Arthurian quest for parts; and all the wonderful people I discovered, who performed the various special services that made the whole thing possible; but aside from being deeply sad, you would also be deeply disappointed. There was only one wonderful person, and that was the man who put the Ron into last month's "Ron's Story." When we got to talking, aside from agreeing we were both happy old tossers who loved bikes, we discovered we had a lot more in common. When we got round to the "What do you ride?" bit, it transpired that Ron also owned an SRX6, and more significantly, that he was considering selling it to provide some cash flow for his Isle of Man trip.

He gave me no idea how lovely his bike was; just that it had the equivalent of about 8,000 miles on it, and that he was considering knocking it out for around a grand. I could make as many plans as I wanted to sort my bike out, but the reality was I still hadn't even named a date to get started. So on a day off over Easter, I arranged to bop down to Godstone and have a look at it. You've seen the pictures! If you like that sort of thing (and I lurv it!) you'll know how excited I was when I saw it. And when I started and rode it, it was everything mine wasn't. Basically, it was a fifteen-year-old new bike with a number of useful improvements.

I left Ron saying I'd have to check my credit status and get back to him. Generally, I try to avoid looking too closely at my finances, because life's pretty sweet as long as I don't dwell on the negatives. However, this was too good an opportunity to miss, so I bit the bullet and started checking all my unopened junk mail looking for a cheap loan offer. Then I came across a thin book of cheques from my credit card issuer, which they'd sent to provide me with extra flexibility for those spontaneous purchases. Clearly, they'd cynically decided they had me on the hook, and all they needed to do was to make it as easy as possible for me to run up plenty of debt. And it worked! As soon as I found them, I called Ron and when he said MBNA would do nicely it was all sorted for the next day.

He agreed that £900 would do the job, as I'd saved him all the aggro of advertising and having to put up with time-wasting wankers coming round; and I rode off as happy as the proverbial porker in poo. The buzz I get from my new partner is very similar to that wonderful excitement you get with a new relationship. Walking out of work after 25 hours and seeing my Yam waiting patiently in the corner, I feel like my new gal has turned up to meet me before walking me home so it's not such a drag. And I love it. After a long weekend away with the family recently, I was aching to get back on the Yam for our daily tryst.

Whether or not this beauty will go the same way as all the others before it, remains to be seen. I really don't want to end up typecast as a pock-marked wife beater in the Tommy Lee Jones mould; I want to show this one how much

I love it and live with it happily for ever and ever. The old one is in a lock up, as my own private breaker. With a little forward planning, I could strip and rebuild the engine from that long before it was needed and that way I'd have a real keeper. Well, I could!

Be careful out there
Carin' Sharin'

We all make Mistakes
TRD issue 49 – September 2001

The events of September 11th overshadowed anything and everything else that happened in 2001, casting a pall over the lives of people around the world and setting in motion a chain of events that continue to have profound repercussions today; both in terms of the wars in the Middle East and the rapid erosion of the human rights, individual freedoms and civil liberties of the population in this country and in the USA

We all make Mistakes

Anyone who's been in the despatch business for any period of time will have their fair share of memories of jobs that have gone arse-up on them for one reason or another. We've all done it. No matter how professional we might think we are, we all have our bad days and occasional lapses. And if there are any smug bastards out there thinking "not me, mate" don't forget it ain't over till the fat bird trills.

Sometimes it can simply be that you're so slick you get ahead of yourself. I remember picking up a serious cheque in Colnbrook, which needed to be taken to a bank in Northumberland Ave and paid in before close of business. I clocked the address and borrowed the customer's phone to call in the details before heading back to town. However, when I arrived in WC2, I opened my pannier and discovered that the envelope was nowhere to be seen. After searching every inch of the bike and myself, I contacted base rather sheepishly. A quick phone call from them to the punter established that it was still sitting where I left it on a desk way out in cargo land. The controller had nobody out west, so I ended up repeating my journey at a ridiculous speed before delivering the goods with minutes to spare.

A category that is always ready to trap the unwary DR is the geographical error. A good example is the time I got all the way from the city, right down through Tooting on my way to a delivery in High Street Malden, before the controller called me to head back to Stratford for a Colchester! Ah, that'll be Maldon in Essex then. (The worst bit was that when I asked him if he was on drugs, it made it obvious how far I had my head up my arse.)

Then there's my mate who famously rode to Cobham in Kent instead of Surrey. I'm sure most of you, even if you haven't done similar things yourself, will certainly have heard some stories.

One of the best (or should I say worst) cases I've heard of was a not particularly bright spark who was given a SW19 pick up going to Gosport in Hants. An hour or so later, when the account in Wimbledon started chasing the job and the rider couldn't be raised on the radio, the controller sent another mobile and waited for a phone call from the police. However, almost an hour after the back up had got the job on board and headed south, the original rider phoned to say he was in Gosport, but he needed them to check the address, because he couldn't find Plough Lane and even the police had never heard of it!

Most balls-ups are nine-tenths inconvenience. Either you double back on yourself or someone else covers the job; but in the end everything usually works out hunky dory and the customer's satisfied, albeit a little disgruntled. However, occasionally a parcel with a high intrinsic value leaps out of an un-bungied topbox and the manure really hits the air conditioning. In 1986, when I was working as the sales rep (plus customer service and general scream chaser) for a well-known courier company, I had to attempt to pacify an extremely unhappy client after a rider had managed to lose a set of slides that they were planning to publish in their magazine. What made this balls-up singularly catastrophic was the fact that the pictures had been taken on a white-water rafting expedition in South America, on a river that had never been successfully navigated before. One rider's bad day resulted in the entire photographic record of the trip being lost forever; and a customer who wasn't in the slightest bit interested in hearing any of the inadequate platitudes I had to offer.

Personally, my greatest *faux pas* happened pretty early on in my career. It wasn't a big deal because the parcel was worth a great deal of money – it actually possessed no financial value to speak of – but it was certainly extremely important. One Wednesday I was buzzing around town doing my usual short hop stuff when I got a call on the radio asking what I'd done with the "blood 'n' guts run" I'd picked up the previous Thursday. This was a regular job going from the Royal Marsden Hospital in Fulham Road to the London School of Hygiene in WC1 and I'd done it loads of times. So I assured Smelly that I'd dropped it at the right place in Keppel Street and carried on with my work.

I knew that I must have delivered it because I hadn't chucked it away and I definitely didn't still have it; but as I rode along a nagging doubt began to develop. The more I thought about it, the less convinced I was that I'd dropped it. Then I remembered. I always worked from my right hand pannier as I kept my wellies, waterproofs, spare spark plugs, and various other bits and bobs in the nearside one. However, when I dragged my mind back a week, I remembered that on Thursday I'd had so much work on that the job from the School of Hygiene had, unusually, ended up in the nearside box along with my Hellys. I realised that I must have knocked out everything from the offside and completely forgotten about the polystyrene container tucked away with my rubberware. I quickly checked to make sure it hadn't been hiding in the bottom all week, but it was conspicuous by its absence.

Then it clicked that the reason the parcel wasn't still sitting there six days later was because I'd called in sick the next day and, as they were always short of roadworthy company bikes, a van had been sent to collect mine. Another rider had used my GT250 on Friday, so by the time I got it back after the weekend, although my waterproof gear was still there, all my other bits and pieces had been removed. I radioed back to base to own up, and suggested that if they could locate my personal stuff, there was a good chance the package would be with it.

I heard Smelly ask Kev what had happened to all two-three's crap and Kev's muffled reply, then a squelch as the transmit button was released. Smelly was hot on radio etiquette and he usually gave a "stand by one" before he went anywhere, but all I heard was silence, so I waited patiently. It was broken by the controller at the mini-cab firm we shared the frequency with. I waited again while he spelled out Oxford Street (including S-T-R-E-E-T) for one of his drivers. After he'd finished, I gave it another thirty seconds before trying a tentative two-three. Nothing. Two-three, two-three! More nothing. Mercury six-two-three, two-three! Two-three, two-three! Zero, zilch and a lot more nuffin. Then the car firm again with directions to Fleet Street.

I decided I'd knock out my next delivery and scrounge a phone when I got there; but as I shot down Walton Street the radio crackled in my ear: "OK, sorry about that folks, normal business has been resumed. Two-three, two-three."

"Two-three?"

"Yeah two-three, knock out your SW3 and RTB."

"Yeah roger… but you know I've still got three W1s and a couple of WCs on?"

"Yeah roger rog. Two-two is waiting for you in Beauchamp Place. Give him your work and get straight back here. Don't stop in Mayfair, don't pass go, and don't collect £200... Which mobile called?"

When I met up with Spike and declined both a cuppa and a race up to Hyde Park Corner, it was obvious there was something seriously bothering me, so he wasn't in the slightest bit interested and wheeled off with a wave, before pulling an illegal right at the Brompton Road. By contrast, I pulled away sedately and rode the same way all the way to back to Warwick Avenue. This was largely because my head was full of thoughts; but also, I think, because unconsciously I was trying to make the most of my remaining time on the orange Suzuki. I knew I'd screwed-up big time and I was probably about to get the bullet; and as I rode into the cobbled mews in W9 thinking it was for the last time, I could feel my stomach cramping with regret. However, as I pulled up outside the office I was met by a couple of creased-up mechanics, who couldn't tell me what had happened for laughing. When I stepped inside it was the same story with the phone room girls; and as I stuck my head through the hatch into the control room, it was an enormous relief to discover that even Smelly was showing off his dodgy teeth. It would seem I was forgiven, he just thought I deserved to sweat a bit for being such a plonker.

I got the full story eventually. It turned out that the Professor at the School of Hygiene had rather belatedly began to worry about the Hepatitis B cultures, which he should have received some six days earlier – particularly as they really should have gone straight back into the fridge as soon as they were delivered. I was largely reliable, whereas the blood 'n' guts run often involved a fair bit of confusion, so Smelly had naturally taken my word for it and accepted that the mistake was at the other end. But after I called back to say I wasn't sure, all that changed. Kev's answer, which had been unintelligible at the time, was: "Yeah, I told one-nine to bung any personal stuff of Dave's in there." Then apparently he swung around on his chair, flipped open the cupboard door he'd indicated, and was confronted by a paperback book, a pair of fur-lined suede gloves and a polystyrene container with "HAZARD" and "KEEP REFRIGERATED" stickers plastered all over it. The sudden silence had come about when Smelly dropped his mike before attempting to trample all over Kev as they both bolted for the door.

They were standing outside trying to decide what to do next when a brand new virgin rider marched up, saying that he'd been issued with a bike and was ready to go. Smelly had looked at Kev for a second before nonchalantly turning to the rider and asking if he had a pen and pad. When the newbie produced them enthusiastically, he was given the address in WC1 before being told, almost too casually, to go into the control room and pick up the parcel in the cupboard that had its door wide open. He was told it would have a Professor X's name on it and that he was to take it directly to him at the London School of Hygiene, and then call in empty on the rider's number.

He walked into the office and returned a matter of seconds later, holding the parcel aloft and waving innocently at the nice controllers, as they stood sniggering twenty feet away with Mark and Martin the mechanics. All four of them laughed and waved heartily as the new boy headed out of the mews on a buckled old pool bike. He probably rode all the way to Bloomsbury congratulating himself on getting a job at such a nice friendly company.

Apparently, he survived his debut delivery without any noticeable side effects and his naiveté intact – which was sweet. Obviously, Smelly had been confident that the container was well sealed and had expected no less; but even back then a good controller was hard to come by, so there was no point in taking unnecessary risks when new riders on shitty bikes were two-a-penny.

I guess if there are any lessons to be learnt from this story they are:

1) Never get ahead of yourself.

2) Always make certain you're heading for the right county.

3) Always check your topbox and panniers before you knock off.

4) Never trust a smiling controller.

Be careful out there
Carin' Sharin'

Terrorvision
TRD issue 50 – October 2001

With as much 70mm of rain falling within a six-hour period, the UK was reeling under what was being described as the worst flooding in twenty years. While a few thousand miles away, less than a month after the terrorist attacks in New York and Washington, the US – with the help and support of the Blair government – were raining high explosive murder on Afghanistan in a vain, vindictive attempt to avenge the deaths of the innocent American citizens who died on September 11th.

Terrorvision

Even if you haven't paid attention to any current affairs since you went on the road (or even longer in some cases), there is absolutely no way you can have missed the reports of the events in the US on the second Tuesday of last month. Assuming that you were working on September 11th, how did you first receive the news from New York? Did your controller break regular 'strictly business' radio policy to announce in an incredulous tone the biggest and most shocking news he or she has ever had to pass on? Perhaps you walked in on a bunch of people watching it on a big screen in a client's reception? Or maybe you saw the drama unfold silently, on a bank of screens in a Granada shop window? If you did, you'd have been forgiven for thinking it was simply another case of super-hype for the latest Hollywood blockbuster.

Did you first hear the news while it was still being assumed that what was being witnessed was simply an appalling accidental tragedy? Do you remember your thoughts when another plane slowly drifted into the second tower of the World Trade Center and everyone watching realised that, for the first time in its history, the US mainland was under attack? Perhaps you were in Canary Wharf, the Stock Exchange, or one of the other areas evacuated when it became apparent that key targets had been hit in the United States and the building you were in could be next. What was your reaction when you were told to leave the vicinity? And what about the men and women in suits?

I'll admit that with the torrent of reaction that erupted on the back of this event, I never really gave a thought to the questions that I've just put to you. As I attempted to assimilate what had happened, you lot just weren't part of the equation. Then last Thursday I came across a *Daily Mirror* supplement, which reported the events of the previous Tuesday with calculated words and spectacular pictures. As I read through it highlighting sections and making notes in the margin (you honestly don't want to ask why I do that, unless you want a very long answer), I came across an item on page 6, which had more resonance for me and my own experience, than anything else I'd read or seen on the subject.

It talked of people fleeing the Twin Towers for their lives and went on to say that, although a lot of them had worked in the colossal buildings for many years, Norman Peat had never been inside before. He had just made a delivery a few floors below the level where the plane crashed and had no idea where the fire exits were. Apparently, he "prayed to God, thought of his seven-month-old son and desperately started trying doors". He got lucky on the third attempt and started down what must have been an unimaginably long stairwell, praying all the way. He lived to tell his tale, but it was only luck (or some would argue the intervention of his God) that separated him from the incomplete list of fatalities. When you consider the sheer scale of the twin towers and think of the number of businesses they must have contained, it's hard to imagine he was the only delivery person in the buildings.

When I started considering things from a courier's perspective, it added a personal dimension that began to grow on me. Imagine what would have happened if on that Tuesday London had been targeted and someone had flown a jetliner loaded with fuel into Canary Wharf or Broadgate. One thing that is inescapable is the reality that if it had happened in London, there's every possibility that a number of you would not be reading this magazine now. Following that line of thinking, if, as a consequence of this country's involvement in the "War against Terrorism", London should become the same sort of target as New York, then many of the streets you ride and the offices you enter will be within the war zone.

IRA bombs (usually with advance warnings by the time they switched to targeting commercial interests) are almost inconsequential when compared with the enormity of what we saw happen to New York's skyline and the thousands of workers in and around those buildings. You would have to be past retirement age to have any memory of the blitz; so few of us can claim to have ever watched live as the familiar landmarks of a major Western city crumbled to the ground with devastating consequences for the people inside. But I'm honestly not trying to alarm you; whatever happens as a result of Bush and Blair's fighting talk, you'll still be infinitely safer in London than the poor folks in downtown Kabul. Nonetheless, can there really be any doubt that if something were to start here in earnest, there would be couriers among the *"collateral damage"*?

Having said that, as you are constantly moving around between possible targets, you would probably be at less risk than the people who work permanently in the buildings – which is an ironic variation on the usual deal. So if everyone who's working in central London is potentially in danger, why am I getting so heavy about it in the Digest? The truth is, although I may be a teenager at heart, who best enjoys writing funny stuff and still gets much too big a bang out of riding quickly through traffic, I'm also a father of four and burdened with an awful streak of responsibility. Consequently, given the enormity of recent events, and more pertinently the reaction to them, there are things I really need to say.

I grew up with the knowledge that in WWII my father was an RAF pilot who flew a Lancaster with Bomber Command. As a kid, I was enormously proud of him and I'm sure that as a much younger man, if the occasion had arisen, I too would have signed up to defend Queen and Country. Fortunately, the necessity never arose; but I'm confident that if it had, my father would have taken me aside and told me much of what I am trying to say now. As it turned out, we never had any sort of serious discussion about any war until after the Falklands when I was thirty. On that occasion we were talking about the sinking of the Belgrano and both agreed that any impartial examination of the circumstances revealed that it was a cynical act, executed in cold blood to prevent the 'Argies' from sailing away from a war that Maggie knew would get her re-elected. My dad then went on to say that wars were never fought for the reasons that we, the general public, are told about; and that if he'd known when he was nineteen what he understood in his later years, far from volunteering (as an instrument maker, he was in a reserved occupation), he wouldn't even have turned up.

So what is this one about? Are the innocent people who died in New York and the Pentagon simply victims of very well organised religious fanatics? Did the hijackers attack the US just because for them it epitomised everything that is evil and wrong with the non-Islamic world? That seems to be the most popular theory at the moment, which is a good 'public consumption' explanation for a number of reasons.

First, it lines up beautifully with the xenophobic stuff that's bread and butter for the tabloids. You know: "It's those completely different people over there wot are the problem – they're mad." Second, and this is even more important, any attempt to question the wisdom of launching a major assault on Afghanistan, can be waved away by pointing to some of the appalling atrocities committed by the Taliban against their own people – particularly women. It certainly seems to be difficult to argue with; but have you noticed how variable criteria (i.e. are they good for business in the West?) tend to be applied to questions of democracy and oppression of the general population. Those of you who do catch the news occasionally will be aware that China (hardly a country renowned for its record on Human Rights) has managed to land the next Olympics! What's that all about?

The more liberal view is that the hijackers took the battle to the American people on behalf of the Palestinian people; or the Iraqi people; or any one of a number of Islamic people around the world who believe that they are suffering daily as a direct consequence of US foreign policy. They point to the indisputable fact that when the Taliban were the freedom fighters and the Russian communists were the oppressors, Bin Laden was trained and equipped by the CIA. Which is of course a similar story to Saddam Hussain's. Back in the day, he used to be a 'goody', who enjoyed US/British patronage and, of course arms – which was not allowed under US and British laws. (But then the US and British governments have always had a flexible attitude to their own laws when it comes to the arms trade. How many of you remember the illegal arms for Iran/financial support for the Contra terrorists episode? It was a scandal for all of five minutes when it broke. And what about the Matrix Churchill 'supergun' affair? How Billingsgate was that?)

When Saddam was stacked up against the anti-Western Ayatollahs of Iran, he wasn't an evil dictator; he could slaughter Kurds with impunity and generate no more by way of outrage than the occasional column inside the *Guardian*. The same liberals will point to all the places in the world today where the local people are being dictated to and oppressed by US-supported regimes. But that's liberals all over, they just muddy the otherwise clear red, white and blue water.

Listening to the radio, I've also heard a wide range of conspiracy theories. There was a serious British think-tanker, suggesting that there was a reason why the CIA apparently had no useful advance intelligence, but were able to trace the movements of the hijackers in great detail within hours of the attack. He believed that the Bush administration were aware that there was a plan to target the US mainland and they decided to allow it to go ahead, because the resultant furore would do for George W what the Gulf War had done for his old man. They knew that military spending cuts would be straight out the window and the Senate would give them a blank cheque (chances are he'll even manage to wangle his Son of Star Wars programme on the back of it). The Institute man was confident that the Bush administration had no idea of how sensational the attack would prove to be, but such a spectacular tragedy presented him with the opportunity to declare a crusade against terrorism and demand the outraged support of the civilised world.

There were various '*Manchurian Candidate*' ideas. One of them suggested that Mossad (the Israeli secret service) had brainwashed stooges to carry out the suicide attacks so they could stitch-up the Arabs. Although it sounded pretty far-fetched, I have to admit the fact that a car was found in an airport car park with a 'How to fly' book in Arabic, a copy of the Koran and a Palestinian passport on the rear seat strikes me as the political equivalent of the police bunging a mask, a striped jumper and a bag marked "swag" in the back of an Escort.

At the far end of the spectrum, where only a few special people can hear the message, there was one of David Icke's devotees, who pointed out that, when read US style, the date of the attacks was 911 – the American version of 999! Which was interesting, but he lost me when he got to the bit about the lizards.

I believe you are in the frontline in more ways than one. In my experience there has always been a degree of crossover between the despatch business and the armed forces – in particular the army. Over the years I've known quite a few couriers who were ex-military, and almost as many again who were considering giving up the road (or actually did) to take the Queen's shilling. With the steady thump of war drums we've been hearing over the last few weeks, I'm sure there will be a number of you who have already considered giving up a game that doesn't seem to be getting any better and volunteering to fight for Tony and George W. All I'm saying is, before you go rushing off, be certain of why you're going. If the honest answer is that you fancy a good scrap in the Khyber Pass, then see the man with the stripes and the loud voice. But if it is because you are outraged by the terrible loss of innocent human life you witnessed in New York, it might be a good time to stop and reflect on what's happened and why, before you rush into anything.

When a man of George Bush Junior's intelligence has control of the most powerful military machine in the world and starts talking like Wyatt Earp, it's worrying to say the least; but when your Prime Minister is nodding along enthusiastically with whatever he suggests, you know you are living in dangerous times. Churchill was quoted as saying that truth is precious, so precious that at times of extreme danger it should be hidden behind a bodyguard of lies. Well for the first time in most of our lives, these really are those times. So I would suggest you take the widest and highest of views, to see if you can work out what's really going on. Then you can decide where the danger originates and the best thing you can do to neutralise it.

Be careful out there
David Gurman

Not so Carin' Sharin'
TRD issue 51 – November 2001

Greek authorities arrested twelve British plane spotters on charges of espionage, after they were accused of taking photographs at an air show at a military base in the south of the country. The eleven men and one woman (a female anorak?) blamed the problem on 'cultural misunderstandings' explaining plane spotting is virtually unheard of in Greece.

Not so Carin' Sharin'

For me, the best thing about writing for this mag is that Roger never tries to influence what I turn in. Provided he thinks it's interesting or entertaining, that it's relevant to the target audience (you, the couriers) and it isn't going to get him sued, he'll run it. When he says at the bottom of page 4 that the opinions and comments of contributors don't necessarily coincide with those of the editor, it isn't just a legal disclaimer, it's also a matter of fact.

Last month when I told him I really needed to write a serious piece about the attacks in the US and that it wouldn't necessarily line up with the tabloid version of things, I felt Roger twitch at the other end of the line. I could just picture him putting his "I'm the editor, publisher and man most likely to be sued or tried for treason" head on, while he desperately tried to straighten up. To his credit, when I explained the courier link, he swallowed hard, set aside all his reservations about the fact that he thinks I'm a dodgy lefty, and said OK.

I always read "In The Saddle", so I'm aware that different people expect different things from this mag. As I said last month, I get most enjoyment from writing the stuff that's supposed to be funny, it's just so much easier to do. I think that's because most of it comes from the nostalgia department and that corner of my mind was never cluttered with the kind of weighty insight I've acquired in the twenty years since my heyday. At the time those memories were being formed I was in my mid-twenties. The portions of my brain devoted to my dick and my throttle hand were as great as the whole of the rest of my brain put together; and while I understood that politics were bogus, I was really too busy having fun to try to understand why.

Consequently, I was generally a happy lad. I thought I had a great job, so I put quite a bit of effort into doing it well. Most of the time, I was the epitome of the polite, reasonable and courteous courier. Crusty, bad-tempered commissioners, who gave their lives in two world wars to earn the right to be bad-tempered with cocky little shits like me, rarely fazed me. It was the same with the snooty, rod-up-the-arse, sour-faced receptionists, who made it abundantly clear that they wouldn't even acknowledge my existence, if it wasn't an unfortunate and extremely distasteful requirement of their job. I could even deal with the occasional pig-ignorant thicko, who was bitter and twisted because he always wanted to drive a train but couldn't get the hang of the steering, so he'd ended up behind a Red Star desk.

Even in my youth, I was always willing to make an allowance for a stranger's personality quirks. In most cases, my unwavering smile and ability to reason a situation through were plenty enough to deal with your average petty-minded tosspot. But when you find a real *Victor Meldrew* on the other side of a desk, he ain't as funny as he comes across on the telly. When you're confronted with someone who is so thoroughly miserable that they devote their entire energy into trying to drag every stranger they come in contact with into their personal emotional black hole, it's hardly surprising that tempers occasionally get a little frayed.

I was speaking to Ian about these situations and he described a classic. Ian was always a very meticulous DR, so when he was presented with an artwork wrapped in brown paper, on one of those appalling days when you've already discovered the limitations of your "waterproofs" by about 10.30, he went out to the bike and got one of the large bin bags he carried for just those occasions. He carefully wrapped the precious load before going back out into the tempest and placing it lovingly in his pannier. Then he firmly fastened the catches and fought his way through aggressive traffic, on roads that were absolutely treacherous, before squelching into an ad company reception and placing the pristine package on the desk.

Or rather, it was almost pristine. The receptionist picked it up by a corner, held it at arm's length as if it was smeared with dog's turd, and sneered in a ghastly South Kensington accent, that she wasn't about to accept it in "that condition!" Ian followed her eyes down her nose and saw a couple of small dark bluey green circles, where his sodden gloves had left the faintest of marks. They were the only indication of the miraculous journey the ad art had survived and he felt a wave of exasperation rush through him. He took the offending article, wiped both sides on his filthy Belstaff, and tossed it back in her general direction, before turning and strolling through the door grinning. He could still hear her apoplectic braying as he rode off.

There were a number of factors, not least of which was feeling like a drowned rat, which combined with the woman's pathetic petty rudeness to push Ian into an uncharacteristic lapse in his professionalism. On a good day, I usually found it easy to smile dumbly in the face of the most outrageous rudeness or patronising behaviour, if that was the line of least resistance; but occasionally my sense of the ridiculous kicked in and whenever that happened I was likely to end up having to be "spoken to" by someone in the office.

I remember in pre-signature days when I was working on wages and me and a couple of other riders were stealing a cuppa and a fag in Shoe Lane cafe. We were sorting our work out between us, when another Mercury rider rode past tooting and raised two then three fingers. I rushed outside and plugged my helmet back into the bike, in time to hear "… Oo-three two-three, two-three two-three!"

"Two-three?" All sweetness and innocence.

Smelly in a pissed off tone: "Where've you been? I've been calling you for ages."

"Sorry Dave, I got caught up with this real pri… pain of a commissionaire in Holborn. I'm just about to do the Printing House Square, which'll leave me in plenty of time for the eleven-thirty in Tavistock Square."

Smooth as silk, without so much as a ripple. Of course he knew I'd been skiving in the cafe and I was lying through my teeth; but as long as I made the effort to come up with a good one, he wouldn't try to dock the allowance we were paid for working through our lunch. It was a power game.

"OK two-three, on your way through, you want…"

I tooted at the other riders in the cafe and sped off. I had my Holborn and the *Times*, Smelly's new one in St John Street, plus two Gray's Inns I'd traded Paddy in the cafe (one of which, he'd taken earlier from Bart in his van) and I had just on fourteen minutes to do the lot if I was going to turn up promptly at the BMA. When I pulled up just round the corner in Holborn, I still had a large chunk of the first minute remaining. I left the GT burbling by the kerb, dashed into the building and tossed the envelope on the desk with a friendly, "There you go mate!"

If I believed in God, I'd have thought it was my just desserts for telling porkies (except that even if He was watching you, lying to your controller probably wouldn't count) because I was half way across the pavement when the commissionaire from hell lumbered into the doorway in full military regalia. He shouted after me, like I was some badly behaved squaddy conscript who needed a good haircut. His braiding, highly polished belt and the three silver embroidered stripes on his arm, all glistened furiously in the sunlight, as he demanded that I deliver it to the company on the sixth floor. I explained that it was a non-urgent press release, and he could keep it on his desk for the next employee who was going up there – even someone coming back from lunch would be fine. But the S'arnt major didn't seem to hear a word I said. He just shouted the same thing a bit louder, like I was a damned Johnny foreigner. So I ignored him and walked back to the bike.

He tossed the A4 envelope at my feet like some sort of W H Smith's gauntlet, and stood with his hands on his hips, clearly relishing the opportunity to put a young lout in his place. I looked at the indignation in his purple face and the veins that throbbed on his temples and I couldn't help laughing. After stamping my feet half a dozen times, like a three year old having a tantrum, I jumped on the bike, turned to face him and went "Nah nah, nah nah, nah!" before sticking my tongue out and dumping the clutch.

As I swung into Gray's Inn Road on amber, I looked back and saw him creaking as he bent over to pick up the job. The saddest part was that he was such a jobsworth that he couldn't simply walk back to his little box and let me take the rap for the undelivered package. As I ducked into Gray's Inn through the out gate, I felt a pang of guilt as I realised that the old soldier had probably given the best part of his life in some pointless war, in some desolate corner of the Empire; but then he should have learned not to fuck with the young and the quick. Especially, when they're down to almost twelve minutes.

My most outrageous over-reaction to obstructive behaviour, came about at King's Cross Red Star at the fag end of a Friday. This was back in the days when ID was a character in a *Carry On* film; but when the Mercury driver at the front of the queue had nothing on him, not even a clip board, to identify him with the company, the man behind the desk wouldn't give him his TBCF (To Be Called For) package. Which was fair enough, if unusual, so Alan was staying calm. He asked the man nicely to take four steps to his left and check out the orange Transit he'd parked right opposite; but he was having none of it and turned to put the large parcel back in the rack. Al looked like he was about to run out of patience, when I stepped forward and said that I'd vouch for him.

The man turned and looked me up and down, before grunting, "And what have you got to say who you are?" That was when I realised that he was either incredibly dense, or simply on a mission to fuck up someone's Friday night. I was shrouded from shoulder to floor in bright orange rubber; on my head I was wearing a matching Griffin Clubman, with a messenger of the gods decal (complete with his distinctive winged helmet) on the side and the tosser was still quibbling. I held up my arms as if I was nailed to a cross and asked him who he thought I worked for; but he insisted that one of us had to bring something into the office with the company's address or phone number on it.

That sorted out one question; he was obviously determined to be as big a pain in the arse as he possibly could. As Alan continued arguing with him, I went outside, started my trusty GT, and rode it through the floppy plastic strips, into the collection office. I pointed to the phone number on the pannier and suggested he get it down quick before the whole place fogged up with blue smoke. This seemed to amuse most of the queue, so I burned out the back tyre for an encore. The human haemorrhoid grabbed a phone and started punching numbers. When he got through and started hollering into the receiver, I slid the back wheel around and rode back outside so he could hear himself scream.

When I walked back in through the smoke, like Clint in *High Plains Drifter*, he was still bellowing into the phone. He pointed at me shouting, "That hooligan rode his bike all around my office!" as if I'd done some sort of trials thing on his counter. I put the scrap of paper with the details of my pick-up in Al's hand and strolled back out as he said to the steaming Red Star man, "Don't forget to check if I work there, while you're on to them."

Alan came outside a few minutes later, grinning broadly and carrying both parcels in his thick arms. He laughed as he reported that the flunky had told him that he'd spoken to my boss: a "Mr Lochead" and I was going to be in BIG trouble when I got back to the office. I'd already spoken to Kev. He called me on the radio as soon as he got off the phone, wanting to find out all the details; but his tone definitely struck me as more amused than outraged, which was hardly surprising considering he was only my boss because everyone else had already slipped off to the pub.

Remember, a professional courier should endeavour to be sensible and courteous at all times; but when all else fails it's best to be childish. It might not resolve the situation, but at least you'll have a good laugh about it later with your mates.

Be careful out there
Carin' Sharin'

Tyre Chi
TRD issue 55 – March 2002

A 43-year-old woman identified only as Miss B, who was paralysed from the neck down after she suffered a burst blood vessel a year earlier, applied to the court for the legal right to demand that the (unnamed) hospital where she was being cared for, should turn off the ventilator she required to keep her alive. In a decision that had pro-lifers protesting vigorously at the message it sent out, Judge Dame Elizabeth Butler-Sloss granted Miss B's wishes. Meanwhile the Queen Mum required no such legal wrangles to shrug her coil off, dying peacefully in her sleep at the age of 101.

Tyre Chi

Roger came up with the title for last month's piece about dogs licking their R1s; and I've gotta say, having re-read it, I thought "a bit of bollocks" was just about spot on. Even I found myself wondering what it was I'd been trying to say. I started off describing my attempts to apply the Taoist 'Way' to my daily life; and ended up getting into childish and "not very Zen" situations with mega bikes. Besides pointing out that it was the philosophical equivalent of mixing my metaphors, any serious student of Taoism or Buddhism would also gently underline that every time I allow myself to be embroiled in such pointless competitions, I'm simply illustrating that I've completely missed the point.

However, in my experience, the great thing about devotees of Eastern religions / philosophies, is that they are unlikely to write smug sarcastic letters to 'In The Saddle' saying: "Oi, Gurman No! You old tosser, you've completely missed the point!" Anyway, the whole point is that I haven't missed the point. I know how I'd like to behave, I just haven't quite got the hang of always managing to apply it in practice. It's like smoking cigarettes: I know how bad they are for my health; that they make me stink; that they're ridiculously expensive and I should just quit. So why am I still smoking? In the same way, I'm aware that I should simply move aside and leave the more aggressive rider to explore his own 'Way'; the trouble is, if my goal is personal perfection, I know that I'm still deep in my own half.

I don't claim to be the greatest thing ever to hit traffic-congested tarmac either; although reading back, I couldn't help thinking that may have been precisely the notion I created. I had visions of young shit-hot gunslingers who'd read my article and were now spending hours simply criss-crossing the route I described, in the hope of finding me and making me eat shit and exhaust fumes on home turf. Worst of all, I knew that if and when it happened, the hotshot was certain to wheelie off afterwards, like a modern day motorcycling equivalent of Clint spinning his Colt round his trigger finger, before holstering it and spitting tobacco juice on my forehead.

So I'd like to backtrack a little. I'm aware that last month I may have given the impression that I thought I was some sort of cross between the Dalai Lama and Carl Fogarty, and the best I can say in my defence is that it just goes to show what a confused ramble it was. Originally, it was a short letter to Roger sneering at "Lifestylers" pulling wheelies; but he liked it and asked me to write a bit more so he could run it as an article. Rather than just bung in a shitload of adjectives and scattering of bigger words to pad it out, I tried to add a little depth by chucking in some background about my daily journey through life and "the route I practise my motorcycling Tai Chi on". I suppose I was hoping it would provide some sort of counterpoint to my later rant; but if it illustrated anything, it was the undeniable fact that, in spite of my best intentions, there's still a strong adolescent streak in me.

The other inescapable conclusion is that whenever I try to write about ideas from the Orient that originate any further east than Leyton, I'm on pretty shaky ground. Around this time last year, I wrote "The Tao of Despatch" in an attempt to pass on *Winnie the Pooh's* version of Taoism; but I got in a right mess and I couldn't even spell the damn bear's name correctly (sorry Rog's Mum). The problem is, I'm a North London boy, living in the South, who's trying to get his head round the East, while he's caught up in the western capitalist system; and before I've even got myself sorted, I'm trying to pass my wisdom on to you. Which is just a teeny bit optimistic considering that half my ideas came from Kwai Chan Caine (well known purveyor of primetime TV philosophy, occasional Shaolin monk, and regular disher out of Kung Fu slappings) and most of the rest come from an upbeat piece of yellow fur fabric with a penchant for honey!

However, in spite of, or perhaps because of my past failures, there are still things I'd like to say about the idea of Motorcycling Tai Chi. A couple of months ago, Lois wrote an excellent piece on "Stress". Central to her theme was a wonderful substance I'd never heard of called 'Noradrenaline'. Among Nora's many other amazing benefits, Ms Lane listed a couple – "near supernatural alertness" and the "expansion of time", which I immediately linked to the apparently superhuman feats performed by master martial artists. It was good to have a scientific explanation for a phenomenon that I first encountered during my cherry-breaking bike accident 27 years ago; but the scientists merely identified something that I had already experienced. I'd also hazard a guess that the Chinese had already learned how to harness the staggering potential of the body's magical secretions a good few thousand years earlier.

Most of you will have had personal experience of exactly the sensations Lois described; so I'm sure you'll have no problem accepting the principle that your hormones possess the ability to expand time when necessary. But what you do with that time is the crucial bit. When I had my first smash, I was amazed to discover that I had all the time in the world to sift through my options; but as my experience was negligible, they basically boiled down to holding onto the bike, or letting go of it. I remember spending an age watching the orange shards from my indicator dawdle past my left shoulder, before making completely the wrong decision and sliding down the road with a hot petrol-leaking bike on my left leg. Among the significant lessons I learned that day, the most important was to never do that again.

The next time I found myself in a full-on adrenaline rush situation, as I floated slowly towards danger in a time warp, I had loads more options to consider; and I actually managed to survive intact. Nonetheless, in my first few years I was guilty of some incredibly stupid and fundamental errors; and too many of them finished with me on the tarmac. Every time I arrived home safely from a day's despatching, or a bit of Hyde Park to Peckham silliness, it was always with the certain knowledge that I had survived because I'd got away with it again, rather than as a result of my consummate skill on two wheels.

This was largely because, from the first time I got on a bike, just about the only thing I was interested in was how to go faster. I probably reached my peak, from a sheer lunatic speed point of view, a few years into my despatch career. This was an extended period when I was regularly riding right on the edge. Whether I was working or not, I seemed to be constantly travelling at insane speeds in relation to the law and the rest of the traffic (not to mention the potential physical dangers). I'm not sure when I finally stopped exploring the boundary between luck and judgment. It was almost certainly after my first child was born (which unfortunately means it was also after I sold my Ducati) but once I recognised it existed, it had a profound effect on my riding. Somewhat belatedly, I realised that I was already way too fast for public roads; and as I didn't have any plans to hone my skills at the limit on the racetrack, it was about time I started improving the rest of my riding.

The most amazing thing was that the moment I began to back off, instead of being constantly reminded of my limitations, I was suddenly impressed by the scope of my capabilities. Whereas previously I'd relied on the sheer intensity of the ride to ensure my progress at the ragged edge, once I changed to a slower, more refined mode, I discovered that I was covering almost the same amount of ground but with infinitely less wear and tear to man and machine. I bought a copy of *Roadcraft* and wasn't especially surprised to discover that most of it was the stuff I'd already learned the hard way; but when I began consciously considering its rules on every journey, everything became smoother and the heart-thumping moments rarer.

Long before I came across Pooh-ist Taoism, I'd assimilated everything *Roadcraft* had to offer and generally felt quietly confident on a bike. Then I began reading about a philosophy that was formulated over twenty-two hundred years before the first motorcycle hit the road and I realised there was another whole level beyond the trusty police handbook. What I call 'Motorcycling Tai Chi' is my way of striving for that level.

Every time I take a journey on a bike, I do my exercises. Instead of carelessly pushing the envelope at outrageous speeds around innocent bystanders, I perform my Tai Chi workout at a far more reasonable pace. My aim is to ensure that although riding a bike is second nature, every decision or manoeuvre I make comes about as a result of a conscious and concise thought process; and, furthermore, that I execute them with pinpoint precision. The idea being that any time it all starts getting heavy, I've got a thoroughly rehearsed repertoire of options to choose from and plenty of time to do it in. Vehicles, traffic islands, and obstructions are an intricate shifting matrix; but when I'm thoroughly tuned in to the flows and eddies on the road it all makes sense. *Wu Wei* is action in harmony with nature; and when I hit that spot, weaving rapidly and smoothly through that pattern requires no more than a variation of the throttle opening and a shift of the hips.

Adhering to the *Tao Te Ching's* advice and trying to eliminate my desires and aggressive impulses generally allows me to rise above the aggression and blunders of other road users; and an acceptance of life's inevitable changes does the same for my blood pressure, especially in total gridlock or when I blow it at traffic lights. I say 'blow it', because traffic lights are the "Extended Time" gates in life's game of *"Ridge Racer"*. In hurry-up mode, by knowing or checking the light sequence well ahead (including using alternative sight lines, like reflections in windows) and then hitting the gaps and the greens just right, it's amazing what you can achieve in a comparatively sedate cross-town dash.

Besides fluidity through traffic and the increased feeling of security, the most significant payoff for adopting a Tai Chi approach is that occasionally when I'm on a bike and it all feels 'just so', I have an overwhelming feeling that I'm totally at one with the Universe. I can't claim that I've mapped out the route, or that I can get there at will, but every once in a while I'll swoop round a bend and realise that I'm in the foothills of that magic kingdom.

Once I'm there, I feel like Bruce Lee on a bike and know nothing can touch me. Then before I get too carried away with my own omnipotence, I always remind myself that Brucie was killed by a sucker punch, so you can never be too careful.

Be careful out there
Carin' Sharin'

PHD in Life Anyone?
TRD issue 56 – April 2002

The two teenage brothers who were accused of the tragic murder of Damilola Taylor in Peckham in November 2000, walked free from the Old Bailey after they were cleared of 10-year-old's murder. The defendants, who couldn't be named because they were only 16, were also acquitted of manslaughter and intent to rob (although they were sentenced to eight years Youth Custody for manslaughter in an October 2006 re-trial).

PHD in Life Anyone?

There's little doubt that a number of you will have been to university, or that some of you will have gone the distance and are now entitled to stick a few choice letters behind your name. I'm sure there'll even be a few of you who, at one time or another, have actually used your degree, with or without honour(s), to get a job. Perhaps you used your BSc in Existential Yoghourt Farming to get a Civil Service position in the Ministry of Defence; or a Philosophy degree to jump on the graduate fast track as a trainee manager in Woolworths. Whatever you may have done in the past, the likelihood is that if you are working as a courier, nobody demanded to see proof of your academic achievements before you started in your current position.

However, if you did the whole mortarboard and gown thing, it does pose one obvious question: how relevant was your degree to your present employment? Or, more to the point, does any of the stuff you studied and regurgitated between the ages of 18 and 21 help make you a better despatch rider? OK, that's a bit loaded, but I'm honestly not out to have a pop at the further educated, I'm simply attempting to establish a position. I'll admit that in the past I may have carried a sizable chip on my shoulder, but there's nowt like a bit of fast riding to blow stuff away.

When I started despatching, it was the first time I'd ever met and mixed with graduates on an equal footing, and in a situation where academic achievements weren't an issue. Suddenly, any prejudices or assumptions I may have been carrying became irrelevant. There were three criteria by which I measured my peers: their knowledge of London; how they performed on a bike; and whether they were up for a laugh when they dismounted. Anyone who scored well on the last two points was always welcome in our flat in Peckham. Age, sex, sexuality, education, race, class, religious tendencies and all the other shit which so often gets in the way weren't even on the agenda.

Friends who went to university and had a ball always tell me what I missed and how much I would have loved it. OK, there was some work involved; but mainly, it would seem, it was about sharing a crusty flat (where there were always impromptu gatherings and occasional legendary parties), doing drugs, disappearing up your arse about The Meaning of Life and trying to get laid. Now, I'm the first to admit all of that sounds very attractive; but it's also a pretty fair description of my initial three years in the despatch business. As far as I can see, the only difference was that when it was time to go to work, the students got down to their books, while me and my flatmates went and played on motorbikes. Nuff said, as far as I'm concerned. But the killer – and this is where, for me, the whole university sales pitch really falls flat – is that while all the students I know were piling up astronomical debts, I was collecting a brown envelope every Friday, which was fat enough to pay for all my essentials and leave plenty for recreational purposes.

For me personally, university was never even a serious consideration. By the time I was sixteen, the school system had already had over ten years to convince me it had something to offer, and it had failed miserably. Consequently, it never occurred to me to use my leisure time to do loads of homework and revision, so I could pass a slew of O-levels, simply to return to do the same again at A-level, before going on to Oxford or Cambridge. That would have required a minimum of another five years and a whole busload of effort, and I had a life to be getting on with. Besides, the prospectus I got from The University of Life (Life Poly as it was in those days) looked infinitely more attractive and the starting pay was much better!

I arrived at that conclusion over thirty years ago, when I was barely out of puberty. So has the rest of my life been blighted by that short-sighted decision? Has the premature termination of my formal education left me disadvantaged in the world of employment? Considering that I've worked ever since I left school, the honest answer has got to be no, actually. Alright I could have earned more, but I've always had enough to enjoy my life, and the same goes for my four children. So, as I never wanted to be a doctor, lawyer or merchant banker (a particularly appropriate bit of rhyming slang I've always thought), I can't imagine what I'd have done differently. By the time I started in the courier business, I'd been working for seven years. I might not have had any academic qualifications worthy of mention, nor any particular specialist field, but I'd had plenty of opportunity to establish that I could get up in the morning and that I was a good all-rounder who wasn't exactly slow on the uptake. I took to despatching like a duck to Hoy Sin sauce and pancakes, and soon discovered that besides having a brilliant job, I was also in the most educational phase of my life.

On any given day, I could expect to find myself in the London offices of many of the nation's, if not the world's, most powerful institutions. *Lloyds, Goldman Sachs, Disney Corp, the CBI, Rothschild's, Saatchi & Saatchi, Herbert Smith, Shell…* (You could write your own list. They're all pillars of the establishment who, along with the government departments and quangos, still provide the bread and butter for the courier business.) I've never been one for pacing, so whenever I was clocking waiting time, I'd look around for something to read. What I picked up tended to depend on the business the punter was in; but all too often, it seems, I had plenty of time to read interesting in-depth stuff. Whether it was in *Campaign, Lloyd's List, Marketing, The Financial Times* or any of the other specialist publications, it was usually information that I wouldn't have otherwise come across, and it invariably gave me a useful insight into the world I lived and worked in. Being a DR is a bit like having a backstage pass on life. Aside from the massive commercial interests, I could just as easily find myself on a film set; the studio of a famous artist; a storage room in the V & A; or behind the scenes at a hospital. And every one of those situations presented me with an opportunity to learn something new.

Why does the academic establishment insist on perpetuating the myth that it has some kind of monopoly on the provision of knowledge? And if its central aim is to impart wisdom to its students, why doesn't it simply confine itself to that? Why does it insist on using examinations and tests to grade pupils, when an assessment of their course work would be much fairer and provide infinitely more useful information? The answer to all these questions is pretty straightforward really and the clue is in that magic word 'monopoly'. Academia is in an incredibly powerful position, whereby it can endorse, or otherwise, your suitability for well-paid employment. Consequently, as "an education" can be your ticket off the breadline, they can afford to demand that you jump through a few hoops. That's where examinations come in. They're pretty arbitrary, really, and completely ignore the different ways people react to tests; but that doesn't matter, because it's never been about discovering who's brightest or cleverest; exams are simply an expedient way of short-listing all the people who'd prefer not to do a crap job.

The biggest con about the whole education system is that when Joe or Jo Average leaves university and starts looking for that pot of gold at the end of their self-financed educational rainbow, they discover that the First Class honours degree, which they sweated blood and bought their own books to achieve, comes a poor second to connections. That Prince Edward and a thousand dullards just like him have already been lined up for all the best gigs. But as long as Mr or Ms J. Average BA understands and accepts how it all works, they'll be given a shot at avoiding the minimum wage. Because if a degree does anything, it indicates that the person who achieved it has displayed a firm commitment to the status quo (and no that doesn't – necessarily – mean they spend all their time at uni playing racquet guitar in front of the bedroom mirror).

Nepotism may be the number one scam facing those who choose to go the University route, but for the rest of us, the neatest thing about the Great Academic Swindle lies on the other side of the educational coin. The flip side which suggests that if you didn't finish school, or did badly at your GCSEs, you were an academic failure and consequently not very bright. No surprise then that a lot of folk take this idea to heart and accept that it's only right that they should do a shit job for shit money, while the 'clever ones' get all the good stuff.

The other day, I was helping out on an advertising shoot featuring Wayne, a 26 year old courier. He was being paid model's rates (i.e. a week's DR wages for the afternoon) and in my opinion he was providing damn good value for money. He was a star. Modelling-wise, he delivered everything that was asked of him; but what was interesting about that was that he did so with such consummate ease that it underlined the simplicity of the role, especially when compared with his mainstream work. He's an experienced DR, and it was obvious that his mind worked at a completely different pitch to those of the highly paid folk around him. Throughout the afternoon, he came up with straightforward solutions to the little quandaries he heard the artistic types agonising over; he whipped out his roll of duct tape and sorted out their props; and even made a couple of good artistic suggestions (which they took on board without ever being aware of their source).

Of course, Wayne and I spent a fair bit of time doing that thing that DRs get to be very good at: sitting around smoking while extremely well-paid media types have high-power confabs (except on this occasion we weren't doing it at six quid an hour!). In one of our stand-by sessions, I was talking about the Digest and Wayne admitted that he doesn't read it. Apparently, his reading isn't up to much (a situation which is a lot more common than many of you who read this with ease may realise) as he didn't do a lot of school. However, Wayne believes that, when all's said and done, he (and his family) aren't doing so badly, considering he's riding a company Bandit, and he's on a PAYE salary of 20K a year.

And he's spot on. Within the prevailing structure of our society, there are very few areas in "The Marketplace" where someone who didn't cut it academically can get anything like a reasonable return on their skills, wit and native intelligence. The fact that a DR who's got a lot more savvy than schooling can still earn slightly above the minimum wage simply serves to illustrate what a demanding and potentially dangerous job it is.

Although many in the business justifiably claim that earning a respectable living is becoming increasingly difficult, despatching continues to provide a home for some very intelligent "failures". In essence, being a courier is a very straightforward job – you pick up packages and deliver them. Anyone who can make sense of an A to Z and ride a bike between two points can do it. But those are just the basics. The really good pros are invariably extremely bright individuals, who develop and practise such an impressive array of "transferable skills", that if they wrote them down (tarting them up with all the right "power words") they'd have incredible CVs.

Next time you're waiting around for a "desperately urgent" package, rather than pace up and down while the Aussie temp on reception tries to find Nigel in the wine bar, sit back in some leather and take a gander at the job section in any of the broadsheets you're sure to find lying about. Skip past the bit that says "Good Honours Degree essential" and check out the person spec for a few of the better paid jobs.

- Must be able to make crucial decisions instantly in high pressure situations.
- Must possess ability to communicate with a wide variety of agencies, at all levels.
- Capacity to manage own workload without direct supervision.
- Willingness to work long hours when circumstances demand it.

Ring any bells?

The decisions you make while you skim through heavy traffic at high relative speeds tend to be a tad more crucial than the average executive finger wringer. After all, what's the worst an exec can do if the heat gets too much and he or she really screws up big time? Lose a shitload of money, or at worst get the sack. It's not even as if they get done for corporate manslaughter (check out the case of Simon Jones who died with a crushed head, less than two badly paid hours into a new job at Euromin in Shoreham docks). In reality, at least half of the monumental decisions the folks on the big bucks have to make hinge on such critical issues as espresso or cappuccino, or whether to go with the Chablis or the Chardonnay.

If you are a serious pro working for one of the big firms, you have to interact with every conceivable stratum of society, right across the entire social and business spectrum (and don't forget that you often have to deal with clients in their homes as well as their workplaces).

The last two points are so bleeding obvious that I won't even bother to comment, beyond saying that in the latter case, it's a question of necessity, because financial circumstances (and bonus schemes) demand that you always work long hours if you're going to have any chance of making a decent wage.

Of course in the real world of employment you can't simply scrub 'round the academic requirements, because it doesn't matter how well you could do it: if you ain't got the paper, you ain't got the job. Consequently, I'm not suggesting that you cash in your transferable skills for a move into a higher tax bracket, simply that you should recognise them for what they are; particularly if, along with me, you were written off as part of The Great Academic Swindle. Because it's all too easy to allow educational snobbery to cause you to underestimate your own intellect, capabilities and worth.

Think about it, the CEOs of all the multinationals, all the academics and intellectuals, and most of the world's politicians, have all been thoroughly university educated. They've had the opportunity to study the accumulated knowledge, wisdom and science (not to mention mistakes) of civilisations from around the world and across the millennia. My question is, if they're all so fuck off clever, why's the world in such a bleeding mess? (answers c/o The Rider's Digest)

Be Careful Out There
Carin' Sharin'

Road Trips
TRD issue 57 – June 2002

Nothing happened in the UK in June that year. However, across the pond the Bush government announced that they had foiled an al-Qaida plot to detonate a radiological or 'dirty' bomb on the American mainland; Lennox Lewis put paid to Mike Tyson's attempt to regain the World Heavyweight title in Memphis, in what was, at almost $107m, the highest grossing pay-per-view fight in history; and Gambino crime family boss John Gotti died of throat cancer, aged 61, in a Federal prison in Springfield, Missouri.

Road Trips

I suppose there must be a fair number of commuters and even a few couriers who ride a bike simply because it's quicker through traffic and cheaper to run than a car. It's not a love thing for them, it's a marriage of convenience; which must be a hell of a life when you think about it. It's bad enough having to struggle up the A2 on a cold wet winter's day if you love bikes, but if they mean nothing to you beyond being an expedient form of transport, it's gotta be soul-destroying.

However, I'm assuming that in your case, as you've chosen to read this magazine, bikes mean slightly more to you than 50+mpg and sixty-five quid a year road tax. The problem is, even if the reason you first chose to ride one was because you got hooked on the sheer joy of two wheeled motoring, it's still all too easy to allow the repetitive negative bits to gnaw away at your passion.

If you commute sixty miles a day, or despatch for fifty hours a week, how do you keep your relationship with bikes fresh? Going back to the human relationship analogy, any agony aunt will tell you that even a marriage that is based on deep and abiding love and affection needs something special from time to time. A little something out of the ordinary to provide a break from the routine and a reminder of what it was that ignited that spark in the first place. Without the occasional explosion of passion on the kitchen table, weekend in Paris without the kids, barefoot paddle in the sea, or good night out with good friends, the whole thing can easily deteriorate into a turgid, soulless grind. And if that sort of thing is allowed to go on for too long, any memories of the bright beginning are likely to slide into a black hole, dragging the prospect of any future joy with them.

Fortunately, bikes tend to provide plenty of opportunities for a "quickie on the kitchen table". Any time I take up the gauntlet and get involved in playing silly buggers through the traffic or blasting around some twisties, it puts me in touch with why I rode a bike in the first place. But great as those little blasts can be, they're a lot like the knee trembling "Wham bam, thank you ma'am" sex of my adolescence; and they can't begin to compare with the intensity of passion available to a couple of mature adults away on a consummately dirty weekend.

So does that mean you have to drape your Fazer in stockings and suspenders, and sign in at a B & B in Whitby as Mr & Mrs Smith? Of course it doesn't; don't be so bloody silly. I guess this is where the motorcycles / marriage analogy falls apart. Because nice as a journey may be with the person closest to your heart (or groin), if the whole point of the trip is to arrive at a destination and get down to some serious shagging, chances are you're less likely to be entirely enraptured by the journey. I'm always banging on about the journey being more important than arriving when you're travelling on a bike, but when it comes to the old fluid exchange situation, the complete opposite seems to apply. So how do you get your relationship with your machine back to basics?

Anyone who's familiar with the 1978 *National Lampoon* classic "*Animal House*" will remember that the shit really started flying after the Delta house toga party, and the whole fraternity was put on double triple probation. Did they wimp out and knuckle down? Did they bollocks! They went on a road trip. (OK, given John Belushi's well-deserved reputation for excess and his premature death, it mightn't seem entirely sensible to use his wisdom to illustrate my point, but hell, you can't deny the man knew how to party.) There is nothing like a road trip with a group of like-minded individuals to provide everything that's good about motorcycling.

My introduction was a trip to Porthcawl in the Easter of 1979. Spring had arrived late, on the back of a particularly bitter winter (my first as a DR), and the trip provided the perfect opportunity to celebrate the return of the kind of weather bikes were designed for. Early on Good Friday morning, two Transits (much more convenient than tents and great for breakdown back up) and nine or ten bikes headed off with the sun on their backs.

Away from the constraints of work and London traffic, the ride was completely different. While it was still largely fast and occasionally downright silly, there was the overwhelming distinction that, although we were mostly on company bikes, we were entirely on our own time – and determined to make the most of it. Which we did. We spent the first evening in the Knight's Arms (and joined the United Bikers to ride off en masse past the waiting police). We went for a little scratch around the hairpins of the Black Mountains; and with the Transits parked either end as goals, we enjoyed a great game of football in a field on the Brecon Beacons. The game disintegrated when Big Nick – a man of monumental proportions – took a van to get the ball back after it rolled about a mile down the hill. When he returned he decided that a variation on bull fighting, where his van was the bull, and the rest of us were toreadors/targets, was much more entertaining than trying to chase skinny blokes all over a football pitch that was covered in sheep shit.

Evenings, if I remember, consisted of drinking copious amounts of Brains beer, followed by cocktails in one of the vans. The alcoholic varieties were concocted from the bizarre array of alcohol we'd scrounged up for the trip; and the others were multi-skinned United Nations jobbies (with ingredients from South Africa, Morocco, Jamaica, Lebanon, Thailand and Penge). In spite of our nocturnal excesses, the ride back was every bit as good as the rest of the weekend. When I got home, I couldn't help thinking of the school trips we used to go on right at the end of the summer term when you'd finished all your exams and there was nothing else to do. There was that same feeling of being away with people you see on a daily basis but, for once, without the threat of work interfering with the fun.

And you don't necessarily have to have a big crew for a successful road trip; it's the company and the sense of freedom that's most important. Early the following year, I rose with the alarm at 8am and pulled back the curtains on a glorious spring morning. While I was eating my breakfast, Dave, who had the day off, pointed out that it was too nice to go to work. He suggested that I take the day off as well, we pick up some French bread and cheese, and go for a picnic on our bikes.

I took another spoonful of Frosties and thought it over. "Only if we go to France to get the bread and cheese."

There's nothing like starting out with a tossaway idea, then talking it up until it's an inescapable mission from God. By the time I rang Smelly to ask if I could interest him in anything from the duty free, it had reached those sorts of proportions. I was the overwhelming voice of reason. It was a Tuesday for Chrissake. It was probably the nicest day of the year so far; and coming as it did on the back of about a fortnight of solid rain, everyone at every two-bit company in London and his Superdream was sure to turn in for work...

Smelly stopped me while I still had at least another dozen rock solid reasons why he should search for some light in his dark controller's heart. My clincher was going to be the fact that as I wasn't much of a 'bread head', my goodwill was worth infinitely more to the company than the few poxy quid I was likely to earn it on a day like that. But I never got that far, because he cut across me to say "OK, call me in the morning... Enjoy it."

Just like that. It was freaky. It was as if it really was a pre-ordained mission and God had indeed been moving in mysterious ways. We went along the landing and Dave kicked Ali's door violently, while I shouted God's instructions through the letterbox. It was sure to be OK for Ali to skive off for the day, because he was a student and that seemed to be the way it worked. More importantly, he was studying photography; and me and Dave both agreed that as God had been good enough to set the whole thing up, the least we could do was get him some decent snaps for the next edition of the bible.

So it was that by 10am the three of us were sailing past Falconwood with the throttles on the stops; brothers sworn to a sacred quest for fresh baguettes et fromage. Now I'm no Chaucer, so I can't really do credit to our pilgrims' progress; but fair play to Ali for standing on the back pegs of my GS425 to take a memorable shot as we galloped along a clear ribbon of A2. It was cheaper and easier to cross without the bikes, so we parked them up in Dover and hovered straight over. While my peers sat in steamy cafes, washing limp Sunblest sandwiches down with dishwater tea and moaning incessantly about the lack of work, we were sur le continent getting stuck in to the plat du jour and toasting "friends across the water!"

In courier mode, if I came up empty in one of the channel ports, the ride back to Peckham would've been a real grind. But in the wee small hours of Wednesday morning, as we walked back to the bikes after a top day's 'French leave', it was with the knowledge that there was still a little more pleasure to be squeezed from our trip.

Less than twelve hours later, I was sitting inside Shoe Lane cafe, trying to look like someone who actually gave a toss, as the assembled riders moaned and whinged about the appalling day they'd had while I was skiving off. In the end, rather than get a good kicking for laughing out loud, I hit the mute switch in my head and just sat there watching their lips moving. They reminded me of a load of pot-bellied married men, sitting in the pub bemoaning the fact that their Doris, Daphne or Deirdre doesn't turn them on any more.

Keep your love of motorcycling fresh, or you risk letting a good thing drift away. Change your undies daily; and have a little change of scenery at least as often as you change your oil.

Be careful out there
Carin' Sharin'

What is a Biker?
TRD issue 58 – July 2002

An absolutely awful month for Russian aviation: first a Tupolev Tu-154 collided with a Boeing 757 over south west Germany killing all 69 people on board the Tupolev (mainly Russian children) and the two pilots on the Boeing; then only twenty-six days later a Sukhoi Su-27 fighter crashed into the crowd at an airshow in the Ukraine killing at least 78 people.

There was an entirely different kind of tragedy for the US population when their House of Representatives passed the Homeland Security Bill.

What is a Biker?

Someone recently described me as "Dave the biker" and I must admit, I couldn't help but feel a tiny frisson of pride. Why? What did I think he meant? Wasn't he simply using the fact that I employ a bike for daily transport to single me out from the other Daves? Surely if that was the case, I'd have been "Dave who rides a bike", or more straightforwardly "Dave the slaphead!"

I was definitely left with the impression that rather than making a simple external observation, he was actually expressing a far more fundamental statement about me. Assuming that was his intent, I couldn't help wondering what the word meant to him. When he used the word 'biker', surely he wasn't lumping me in with a group that encompasses everything from pizza 'peds to R1s and beyond, because that's a big generalisation. I've established that I'm into inclusion, but even a wishy-washy liberal like me wouldn't propose that everyone who fits that bill is a 'biker'.

My Concise Oxford Dictionary says: "Biker / n. a cyclist, esp. a motorcyclist." So a Biker is by definition anybody who rides a two-wheeler – in particular, if they get a bit of help with the pedalling.

If my attempt to be precise proved anything, it was that some words acquire a meaning that goes way beyond the dictionary definition. If you stopped someone and asked what a biker is, most could muster a more precise description than the C.O.D. but in reality, their answers are more likely to offer an insight into their personal views and prejudices than to provide any real clarification.

To a *Daily Mail* reader, 'biker' probably conjures up a frightening image of a cross between a Hell's Angel and Marlon Brando in *The Wild One*. Women around the Home Counties and shires live in mortal fear of drug-crazed animals on motorbikes. You've seen them peeping round their nets as you ride through their tranquil villages, telephones clutched tightly in hand ready to dial 999 as you pass. So Middle England's response is unlikely to tell you anything useful; and as far as insight into the respondent's views go, you'd learn as much if you asked "How wonderful was the Queen Mum?" or "What percentage of black people do you think are muggers?"

So let's ignore what Joe Public thinks because they're notoriously unreliable. What do I think makes a biker? One thing I can state with absolute certainty is that when I bought my first bike there was no way I'd have described myself as a biker. But twenty-seven years down the line, I'd defy anybody to challenge my right to the epithet. While in my book it's not simply a question of whether or not you ride a bike, I still can't provide a nice neat definition. However, I'm hoping that a ramble around my experience will offer some illumination.

I bought my first bike, a TS90, when I was twenty because I was sick of the vagaries of public transport and of spending an hour and a half on a journey that would take 25 minutes on the Suzuki. At least, that was the reasoning I presented to my newlywed wife. In reality, I was struggling to maintain a reasonable voice and a poker face because the whole truth was that I'd been enchanted by bikes since I was a kid.

In the sixties, you couldn't turn on the bank holiday news without seeing black and white images of teenagers in parkas swarming over groups of black leather-jacketed bikers. The 'Rockers' always seemed to be woefully out-numbered, so partly I was routing for the underdog; but more significantly, their choice of machine left the Mods out in the cold. I never understood whether all the mirrors were due to paranoia (because they knew they had targets on their backs) or to make their scooters resemble beauty salons, because the motors sounded like hairdryers. By contrast, the Rockers' cafe racers were rolling thunder; and instead of a mass of pointless frippery, they had useful additions like ally tanks, bikini fairings, and hand-milled rear-sets.

But I was never part of a biker crowd when I was young. In my teens, the closest I came was when I narrowly missed the "good-humoured" kicking my mates got from *The Devil's Henchmen* (after they'd wound up the consciously crusty bikers by chanting "soap and water" at them – then failed to make good their escape). When I bought the Suzi, aside from a friend who rode his CD185 to work, I was the only person I knew who owned a bike.

A few years earlier, Pete's Benly was the first bike I'd ever attempted to ride. In the car park at the back of the Chemistry Department in UCL, I dropped the clutch too quickly, snatched the throttle back in panic and stuffed it into the back of a VW camper! When I bought my bike, it was over three years after the debacle in the car park. I'd embarrassed myself so badly on that occasion that I hadn't even attempted to ride one since. In 1975, there was no such thing as a CBT – as long as you had the readies and a provisional, you could ride off on anything up to 250cc. Except me, that is, because I couldn't get the hang of the clutch.

A fourteen-year-old came out of the workshop to demonstrate and then stood by and watched as, mindful of my flying start on the Honda, I fluffed it time and again. When I finally managed to wobble for a full turn of the wheels without stalling, I tossed a wave and stuttered up the road. I stalled at the next give way line, but I was out of sight of the shop by then, so I didn't have to listen to that acne-faced little fucker giggling again. It was the same at the traffic lights, and half a dozen more times before I reached home three miles away. For a couple of days it was a nightmare. Largely, this was because I wasn't entirely sure if it had three or four gears, but when a friend of my brother's took it for a spin and informed me it had five, things began to get easier.

Nevertheless, before I'd owned it for a month, I'd notched up a speeding endorsement and had my worst-ever smash. I was on a steep learning curve and I knew I needed to climb it PDQ if I was going to have any chance of retaining life, limb, and licence. Fortunately, I started a new job soon after and two of my colleagues and all of their mates owned bikes. Phil pointed out the sagging chain and showed me how to adjust it, while the others drew my attention to various shortcomings in my roadcraft ("You ride like a total wanker! I can't understand how you stay on the bike!").

On one of the first scorching days of 1976, while riding in short sleeves, I threw it away on a hot greasy bend, and ended up bike-less throughout the best British summer in living history. This wasn't as a consequence of my injuries, but because my wife, who had twice seen her favourite body nastily bashed and gashed, had threatened to cut off my goolies while I slept if I so much as mentioned the B word again. It was the end of '77 before I felt able to broach the subject without fear of becoming eligible for harem work. I got a CG125 so it was absolutely clear that I'd bought it simply because it was the most practical way of getting from Clapton to Woolwich and back.

Yeah, right. I passed my test the following spring, and my wife and I agreed to separate later the same evening. I'm not suggesting for a minute that it was all about bikes but there's no denying that, as last straws go, it was an extremely bulky one. Single, and with no reason to keep the pretence up, within a couple of days I'd part-exchanged the little four stroke for a Yamaha YR5.

The YR5 was the precursor to the RD350 and was a pretty rapid bike in its day. Compared to anything else I'd swung my leg across, it was wickedly fast. The handling, with standard Yamaha shocks and Teflon Bridgestones, fell some way short of awe-inspiring, but if you kept it in the sweet spot, the rasping acceleration was quite the opposite, and the twin-leading-shoe front brake was far more effective than any of the Jap discs at the time (who remembers 'wet lag' when it really meant something?). Besides, I could always produce sparks on roundabouts, and remember scaring more than one rider on a larger bike into submission (including a memorable joust I had right across Islington and Hackney with one of those posh new GS750s).

Throughout that summer, I fixed one thing after another on the Yamaha – then it was stolen. With my bike gone and my marriage in tatters, I ran away to America to build a new life; and within days of arriving in Boston, I was offered an immaculate Norton Commando for a very reasonable price, which was just a little under my entire cash reserve. I agonised over it for a week but by that time my kitty had dwindled below the asking price, so it wasn't an option. That was probably a good thing because, as it turned out, it was only a few weeks later that I was reduced to eating leftover pizza and boxes of donuts from a friend who owned a franchise.

I returned barely two months after my dramatic farewell, with no bike, no job, no money, and nowhere to live – except with my parents. A friend told me about a despatch company that supplied its riders with bikes and equipment, but I thought it was an urban myth. However, living back at home with mum wasn't ideal at that stage of my life, so I rang Mercury the same day. I assumed that if they really existed they'd have a waiting list that stretched into the mid-eighties, but less than a week later I rode out of the mews as a genuine motorcycle courier.

But I knew I was bogus, because although at 24 I was among the oldest in my peer group, most of my *compadres* had been riding bikes for years, some since they were toddlers; whereas, if you added up the sum total of my experience, it amounted to little more than a full year and a few thousand miles. I had more front than Selfridges, so no one really noticed it, but my insecurities around my lack of pedigree nagged at me for years. In spite of the respect my new vocation generated among other motorcyclists (including British bikers who in those days were notoriously snotty about pilots of "Jap crap" – particularly two-strokes), I felt like a new boy. After three winters as a DR, I treated myself to a Ducati 900SS and even the Harley riders waved to me, but there was still that voice in my head muttering, "Fraud!"

I realise now that I set the bar unrealistically high and that I was being way too harsh with myself, but for me the word 'biker' has always had a special connotation. As I said at the top, I don't normally favour exclusivity, but my parameters are considerably narrower than the dictionary definition. It doesn't include the teenager who buys a 'ped until he's old enough for a Corsa. Nor does it embrace the mid-lifer who's traded in the wife and family for a young blonde, an Audi TT and an R1.

A biker isn't just passing through; he or she is along for the whole ride. There's an adage along the lines of, "If you're not a socialist in your twenties, you have no heart, but if you're still one in your forties, you've no brain." Many non-bikers would probably apply the same maxim to a love of motorcycles. But who gives a toss what they think? What do they know? I'm not suggesting that you need to have been riding for twenty years to qualify. Occasionally, young socialists grow into old ones (but not in New Labour) and it's the same with bikers. You can fall madly in love when you're 18, but it's only after you've reached your golden jubilee that you can state with confidence that it wasn't just a passing infatuation.

A biker is someone who rides through choice. Not because it's the most comfortable way to transport a body, but because it can be the most magical way to carry a soul. With the possible exception of downhill skiing, motorbikes provide the purest, most intense and most accessible means of travelling at superhuman speeds. It's not really about aspiring to get your knee down, or your front wheel up, it's about recognising a bike's ability to keep your spirit floating.

Bikers know that their passion will offer them a continuous stream of life-threatening situations. Recently, there've been many words in these pages about adrenaline and all the body's other goodies, so I won't revisit that ground. I'd simply add that over the centuries many volumes have been written describing the ways that close proximity to death can provide an insight into just how precious, sweet and truly wonderful life can be. When you're on a bike, thundering along the twisting tightrope between life and death, you don't need to have read it, you can feel it!

Then again, when the guy labelled me "Dave the biker" perhaps he didn't even realise that mine wasn't a 'ped and all he meant was that I ride a bike!

Be careful out there
Carin' Sharin'